Messages
from Heaven

~ WITNESSING HEAVEN ~

True Stories of Transformation from
Near-Death Experiences

Messages from Heaven

EDITORS OF GUIDEPOSTS

Messages from Heaven

Published by Guideposts Books & Inspirational Media
100 Reserve Road, Suite E200
Danbury, CT 06810
Guideposts.org

ACKNOWLEDGMENTS

Every attempt has been made to credit the sources of copyrighted material used in this book. If any such acknowledgment has been inadvertently omitted or miscredited, receipt of such information would be appreciated.

"Temporary Home" written by Zac Malloy, Luke Laird, and Carrie Underwood. Lyrics © BMG Rights Management, Universal Music Publishing Group, Sony/ATV Music Publishing LLC. Lyrics Licensed & Provided by *LyricFind*.

Scripture quotations marked (ESV) are taken from the *Holy Bible, English Standard Version*. Copyright © 2001 by Crossway Bibles, a division of Good News Publishers. Used by permission. All rights reserved.

Scripture quotations marked (KJV) are taken from the *King James Version of the Bible*.

Scripture quotations marked (NIV) are taken from *The Holy Bible, New International Version*. Copyright © 1973, 1978, 1984, 2011 by Biblica, Inc. Used by permission of Zondervan. All rights reserved worldwide. zondervan.com

Scripture quotations marked (NLT) are from the *Holy Bible, New Living Translation*. Copyright © 1996, 2004, 2007 by Tyndale House Foundation. Used by permission of Tyndale House Publishers Inc., Carol Stream, Illinois. All rights reserved.

Scripture quotations marked (NRSV) are taken from the *New Revised Standard Version Bible*. Copyright © 1989 by the Division of Christian Education of the National Council of the Churches of Christ in the United States of America. Used by permission. All rights reserved.

Cover design by Pamela Walker, W Design Studio
Interior design by Pamela Walker, W Design Studio
Cover photo by Dreamstime
Typeset by Aptara, Inc.

Printed and bound in the United States of America
10 9 8 7 6 5 4 3

*For the word of the cross is folly to those
who are perishing, but to us who are being
saved it is the power of God.*

1 Corinthians 1:18 (ESV)

CONTENTS

Introduction ix

Experiencing What's Beyond.. 1
  By Randy Petersen

Keeping the Faith... 27
  By Tim Varney, as told to Anita K. Palmer

A Divine Message... 65
  By Beth Praed, as told to C. Hope Flinchbaugh

A Message of Love.. 97
  By Nadia McCaffrey, as told to Anita K. Palmer

Heavenly Messages that Transcend Time and Place............................ 139
  By Charles Taylor, as told to C. Hope Flinchbaugh

INTRODUCTION

But as it is, they desire a better
country, that is, a heavenly one.
Therefore God is not ashamed to be called
their God, for he has prepared for them a city.

Hebrews 11:16 (ESV)

Four ordinary people, from different places, different ages, different walks of life, and different beliefs. Yet all of them share a similar extraordinary experience: a vision, or visions, of heaven that came in that thin place between life and death, between the material world and the spiritual, that brought them to the very portals of heaven—in some cases, more than once.

Beth Praed was a child, just past her ninth birthday, when she was taken to a place of golden light, where she saw a bearded, brown-robed man who asked her a question that changed her life forever. Charles Taylor was working for a natural gas company when he died and saw his own body below him as angels transported him to see Jesus. Tim Varney was a mechanic and truck driver, riding an ATV with his stepson when an accident took him on his first journey to the gates of heaven that gave him new purpose in life. Like Beth, Nadia McCaffrey was a young girl when a celestial vision of her petite *Maman du Ciel* (little Mother of the sky) gave her a ravenous hunger for heaven so strong that she would try anything to return there—and when she succeeded, she was told she couldn't stay. She had a purpose to fulfill.

Why does God give such amazing near-death experiences to some people but not to the rest of us? We might never know the answer, but those who have died, gone to heaven, and live to tell about it return to this life with renewed senses of purpose, a fresh understanding of how precious the gift of life is, and a longing to one day go back to the remarkable place of which they were given a tantalizing glimpse.

While we might never experience anything quite like the near-death experiences (NDEs) recounted in this book, at least in this life, we nonetheless can benefit from what the experiencers, as people who had NDEs are often called, share in their stories. If there is one thing every one of the four experiencers in this book would tell us with absolute conviction, it is that heaven is real and that Jesus is there, waiting for us to join Him one day: "And if I go and prepare a place for you," Jesus said in John 14:3 (NIV), "I will come back and take you to be with me that you also may be where I am."

As Nadia McCaffrey so eloquently put it in her remarkable story, shared in this book:

Death. It is not final. It is not something to be afraid of. The space between *here* and *there*, between life and what we call death, is so thin. I never have found the right words to explain this. You almost can see through it, like a veil. Death is not the end of anything. It's just another level. It's just another place.

In this book, you'll be given the opportunity to peer through that veil, through the eyes of Tim, Beth, Charles, and Nadia, to see just a hint of the myriad glories of the heavenly home God has prepared for us.

May you find your faith strengthened and your heart full of joy as you anticipate the joy of this place where God "will wipe away every tear from [our] eyes, and death shall be no more, neither shall there be mourning, nor crying, nor pain anymore, for the former things have passed away." (Revelation 21:4, ESV)

Experiencing What's Beyond

By Randy Petersen

You see a brilliant light in front of you, above you. It washes out everything else. You are drawn to it. You sense yourself rising, floating. You turn and look down and see a hospital room— and your body lying there. Machines are beeping. White-garbed people are hovering around that body, very concerned about one thing: your death.

But you aren't concerned. You feel peace like you've never known.

You turn toward the light. It seems you're moving through a tunnel toward that radiance. Suddenly you notice people along the way, people you used to know when they were alive. They have all passed on, and now they're gathering to cheer you forward.

Then you encounter one person in particular, someone who left your life too soon. Issues remain unresolved, important things unsaid. It's a father who walked out on the family, a mother taken by cancer, a favorite teacher or best friend.

In this moment of overwhelming love and light, they speak to you. And what do they say? Is it explanation, forgiveness, challenge? Are they welcoming you into a new existence or sending you back to complete your earthly sojourn?

And how will their words change you?

Life after Life

Hundreds, perhaps thousands, of people have experienced something like this. In recent years such phenomena have been widely reported and intently studied. And hotly debated.

In 1975, scholar-author Raymond Moody coined the term near-death experience (NDE) in his landmark book *Life After Life*. There had been previous research on resuscitated people dating back to the 1890s, but Moody found some common threads, weaving them together in this new concept, the NDE.

The last few decades have seen a proliferation of NDE reports.

The last few decades have seen a proliferation of NDE reports, possibly due to medical advances that bring more people back to life after their hearts stop beating. Perhaps as a society we are more open to hearing about experiences like these.

So what happens to people when they die? Specifically, what happens to their consciousness? Those questions put us on the border of science and spirituality. Some scientists seek a material explanation in the imaginative ability of the human brain. But for those who believe in a spiritual reality wrapped around this world like a plush blanket, the idea of our awareness floating into a realm of love and light—well, it's not a stretch.

The Common Threads

Every NDE is unique, but certain details keep coming up in the firsthand reports from those who have journeyed to beyond and come back to their earthly life. Different scholars have slightly different lists of these common factors, but here are those that appear most frequently:

Peace. Though the person knows he is dead, he has a sense of calmness and well-being.

Out-of-body awareness. Experiencers often feel like they're rising up out of their body, shedding their skin as if they're removing clothing, and looking down upon themselves. Some have reported that their consciousness has drifted to another room of the hospital, or even miles away to the home of a loved one.

Moving through a tunnel toward a light. Sometimes it's a cave or staircase, but it's a passageway, often leading to a bright light.

Love. They feel accepted and connected, and their heart overflows to others.

Encounters. In one university study, nearly two-thirds of respondents included a personal encounter as part of their NDE, though the specifics vary widely. Sometimes they meet God or Jesus or other sacred figures, often angels. Some people meet deceased loved ones and have important conversations with them, which might be in an unspoken language.

Life review. An old cliche suggests that people in a life-threatening situation "see their life passing before their eyes."

Some NDEs include something like that. Often in the company of the sacred figure, people remember scenes from the past in which they did good or bad things.

Stay or go? Some have reported a decisive moment at the "gate" of the land of light. They must choose whether to go forward into the afterlife or return to their earthly lives. In some cases the choice is made for them and they are sent back.

The In-Between

Spoiler alert. When we hear stories of people facing that decision to stay in the place of peace and light or to return to their earthy lives, we know what decision was made. They have returned. Otherwise we wouldn't be hearing their stories.

And this raises an important question: *Have they really "died"?* Some scholars are quick to remind us that we're talking about "*near*-death" experiences. These events, as generally related, have taken people to a boundary line of sorts, but they have not crossed it.

> *The near-death experience seems to occur in an in-between space.*

Back on earth, in the operating room or perhaps in the wreckage of a car crash, they might be declared dead. The heart stops, the brain ceases, the machines that measure vitality are registering zero, and so there's ample reason to say that the person "came back from the dead," "died" on the table, or was "dead for fifteen minutes" before resuscitation. But it's still an open question as to whether we should call that "death." Perhaps there are some measures of vitality we haven't discovered yet.

Thus the near-death experience, reported in similar terms by a remarkable number of people around the world, seems to occur in an in-between space. People are declared dead by traditional medical standards and their consciousness seems to travel to the doorstep of heaven—but no further.

Why is this important?

It might help us hold on to a healthy uncertainty about definitions. Often these experiences are described as "going to heaven." They certainly seem heavenly. Peace, love, light, angels, loved ones, perhaps even Jesus are there. But the stories themselves suggest that this is just the entryway to heaven. We might see this as the tailgate party out in the parking lot before the big game.

But do these NDEs show us what heaven will be like when we finally cross that boundary? Maybe. Or maybe heaven will be far, far better—just as the actual game in the stadium exceeds the excitement of the pregame party. We can learn from these reports, but perhaps the best way to put it all into context is to search the Scripture.

Conversation Pieces

What messages are communicated by NDEs? Are there conversations with sacred beings or loved ones? What do these sacred beings say, and how do those "messages from heaven" affect the lives of those coming back from an NDE? What can the rest of us learn?

On that list of common elements of an NDE are three crucial "conversation pieces": love, life review, and "stay or go?"

To hear some NDE returnees tell it, from the moment they shrugged off their physical frames, they were swimming in an ocean of *love*. They felt the peace of being loved and moved through a passageway of some sort to the light of love. When they chatted with sacred beings, they found reassurance that the universe is built on a love that goes beyond anything they've ever known. Conversations with departed loved ones are often comforting, encouraging, and restoring. Forgiveness asked for and offered.

> *Many friends and family members report that NDE returnees come back with a greater sense of purpose.*

It might be hard to square the concept of overwhelming love with the *life review* reported in many NDEs. This is, after all, a sort of final judgment. You would expect criticism and shame during the review of selfish or hurtful choices. But perhaps it's akin to receiving correction from a loving parent or dedicated teacher. You know you're loved, even while your past behavior is critiqued.

The *"stay or go?"* question is another frequent subject of these other-worldly conversations. Many NDE-ers say they have a new purpose. There's something they have to learn yet. There's some relationship they need to restore, some deed they need to accomplish. Perhaps this calling is to take care of another person. We often hear that it's the figure of God or Jesus making that determination: "It's not your time yet. You've got more to do on earth."

And in fact, many friends and family members report that NDE returnees come back with a greater sense of purpose. They're driven.

Some feel compelled to share the secrets of the afterlife, but others throw themselves into service, sharing divine love in the best ways they can.

What Does the Bible Say?

Bible-believing Christians haven't always known what to do with near-death experiences.

The concept of an afterlife is well supported throughout the Bible and through millennia of Judeo-Christian tradition. No problem there. Death is not the end. The Bible says a lot about heaven, about God's future kingdom, and about resurrection—not just for Jesus but for all believers. These are all core elements of Christian faith.

Also, in an ongoing debate with atheism, NDEs provide strong evidence for the existence of God, or at least a spiritual realm beyond the material world.

Still, the experiences make many Christians feel uncomfortable, perhaps because they seem out of the ordinary, not the sort of thing you learned in Sunday school. "I tried to tell my minister," said one NDE returnee, "but he said I had been hallucinating, so I shut up."[1]

And there are certainly legitimate questions to consider. Do the specifics of NDEs line up with biblical teaching? Are we replacing the Bible with NDE doctrine?

"Dear friends," we read in 1 John 4:1, "do not believe everyone who claims to speak by the Spirit. You must test them to see if the spirit they have comes from God. For there are many false prophets in the world." (NLT) Jeremiah warned against false prophets, saying, "They are making up everything they say. They do not speak for the LORD!" (Jeremiah 23:16, NLT)

Some Christians fear that NDEs lead to a "do-it-yourself" spirituality, where you can create your own afterlife the way you want it to be. And if Jesus is just another sacred being on the path to glory, how does that jibe with New Testament doctrine about his unique role as Savior of the world?

And, more to the point of this book, what are we to make of messages received during NDEs? Do we take them as gospel truth, even if they contradict what the Bible says?

These are important matters. So let's look at a few specific Bible passages and some general biblical concepts.

The Apostle Paul

Paul faced more than his share of danger. Early in his career, in the town of Lystra, some enemies stirred up a mob against him:

The biblical story of Paul's conversion is another candidate for an NDE.

"They stoned Paul and dragged him out of town, thinking he was dead. But as the believers gathered around him, he got up and went back into the town . . . ." (Acts 14:19-20, NLT)

That sounds like the start of a near-death experience report, but we have no more info about that occasion. Still, it's fascinating to read what he later wrote to the Corinthians.

I will reluctantly tell about visions and revelations from the LORD. I was caught up to the third heaven fourteen years ago.

Whether I was in my body or out of my body, I don't know—only God knows. Yes, only God knows whether I was in my body or outside my body. But I do know that I was caught up to paradise and heard things so astounding that they cannot be expressed in words, things no human is allowed to tell.

(2 Corinthians 12:1-4, NLT)

This also sounds like an NDE, but I should tell you right now, the math doesn't add up. The incident in Lystra happened eight or nine years before he wrote the letter, not fourteen. Yet we know Paul was frequently attacked. A few verses earlier, he says he has been "often near death." (2 Corinthians 11:23, NRSV) Could he be writing about another occasion when he apparently died and came back?

The "third heaven," if you're counting, was beyond the cloud sky and the starry sky—the place where God lived. And while the messages given to Paul in that "third heaven" encounter were classified, perhaps they informed the content he preached and wrote later to the churches he started. A few verses later, he shares a bit of divine wisdom. After praying for the healing of a physical problem, he hears (or remembers?) the Lord saying, "My grace is all you need. My power works best in weakness." (2 Corinthians 12:9, NLT)

The famous biblical story of Paul's conversion is another candidate for a near-death experience. On a trip to arrest members of the Jesus sect in Damascus, Paul (then going by the name Saul) was knocked to the ground. He saw a bright light from heaven, in which Jesus appeared, saying, "Saul, Saul, why do you persecute me?" (Acts 9:4, NIV) The injury was serious enough that he was blinded for several days.

Could we read this account as an NDE? An accident resulting in possible brain injury. Seeing light. Seeing Jesus. Hearing a message that sounds like a life review. And in the aftermath of this event, Paul received a new calling. He was driven to share the message of Jesus beyond the Jewish world.

In case you're wondering, this Damascus Road story doesn't fit the "fourteen-year" timeline either, but it's another tantalizing example from the life of an important biblical figure.

The Patriarch Jacob

Visions and dreams are common in the Bible. Most of them don't connect with an apparent death or a near-fatal injury. (One exception, besides Paul, is the early Christian martyr Stephen in Acts 7:55-56, who was being stoned to death when he had a vision of an exalted Jesus.)

Visions and dreams are common in the Bible.

Yet other biblical visions have details similar to the reports we hear concerning NDEs. Jacob had two.

As he ran away from home, escaping the wrath of the brother he had just cheated, Jacob dreamed of a stairway to heaven (Genesis 28:10-17): "And he saw the angels of God going up and down the stairway."

From the top, God spoke a message of blessing and covenant: "I am with you, and I will protect you wherever you go. One day I will bring you back to this land."

After awaking, Jacob exclaimed, "What an awesome place this is! It is none other than the house of God, the very gateway to heaven!"

Years later Jacob returned to the area and prepared to face his estranged brother, Esau. During a fitful night, he had another dream, in which he wrestled with a mysterious being (Genesis 32:22-32). The biblical text describes this being as "a man," and Jacob was convinced he had "seen God face to face." In the encounter, Jacob was given a new name.

Though Jacob sustained a serious hip injury, he survived this encounter. It's unclear whether he was ever near death, though his opponent did say, "You have fought with God and with men and have won." Was this actually a near-death experience, in which Jacob fought his way back?

We don't know that. Still, in both of Jacob's dreams we find NDE-like details. The "stairway" is a passage into a heavenly place where God is. There are angels moving through it. Jacob calls the place a "gateway to heaven," which is a great term for the "in-between" location of NDEs. Later he has a close encounter with a being who is sort of human and sort of divine. Like many returning from NDEs, he receives messages about his future and his identity.

The Prophet Isaiah

The story of Isaiah's calling (Isaiah 6:1-8, NLT) also bears a number of similarities to the accounts of modern NDEs:

It was in the year King Uzziah died that I saw the LORD. He was sitting on a lofty throne, and the train of his robe filled the Temple. Attending him were mighty seraphim, each having six wings. With two wings they covered their faces, with two they covered their feet, and with two they flew. They were calling out to each other,

"Holy, holy, holy is the LORD of Heaven's Armies!
The whole earth is filled with his glory!"

Their voices shook the Temple to its foundations, and the entire building was filled with smoke.

Then I said, "It's all over! I am doomed, for I am a sinful man. I have filthy lips, and I live among a people with filthy lips. Yet I have seen the King, the LORD of Heaven's Armies."

Then one of the seraphim flew to me with a burning coal he had taken from the altar with a pair of tongs. He touched my lips with it and said, "See, this coal has touched your lips. Now your guilt is removed, and your sins are forgiven."

Then I heard the LORD asking, "Whom should I send as a messenger to this people? Who will go for us?"

I said, "Here I am. Send me."

What do we see here? A vision of the Lord in glory (and probably dazzling light). We know the Jerusalem Temple was rectangular, something like a passageway, with the Holy of Holies, where God would be, at one end. There are angels around. Isaiah goes through a sort of life review. He admits he is "filthy," but there is an encounter with an angel, who offers cleansing. Then Isaiah is sent back with a new sense of purpose.

> *What do we see?*
> *A vision of the*
> *Lord in glory.*

King Saul and the Prophet Samuel

In one of the more interesting stories of the Bible, King Saul receives a message from his deceased mentor, Samuel.

In 1 Samuel, we read that Saul was losing a war with his archrivals, the Philistines. The Lord wasn't answering his prayers for guidance, and so he took drastic action. He sought out a medium, though he himself had outlawed such practices. In disguise, he ventured out to the home of a woman who could contact the dead.

Finally, the woman said, "Well, whose spirit do you want me to call up?"

"Call up Samuel," Saul replied.

When the woman saw Samuel, she screamed, "You've deceived me! You are Saul!"

"Don't be afraid!" the king told her. "What do you see?"

"I see a god coming up out of the earth," she said.

"What does he look like?" Saul asked.

"He is an old man wrapped in a robe," she replied. Saul realized it was Samuel, and he fell to the ground before him.

"Why have you disturbed me by calling me back?" Samuel asked Saul.

"Because I am in deep trouble," Saul replied. "The Philistines are at war with me, and God has left me and won't reply by prophets or dreams. So I have called for you to tell me what to do." (1 Samuel 28:11-15, NLT)

The response was not favorable for Saul, whose disobedience had alienated the Lord. Samuel predicted that Saul would lose the upcoming battle and be killed, along with his sons. They'd all be "here with me," Samuel said, in the place of the dead. And it happened just as he prophesied.

> *Communication in near-death experiences is almost always non-physical.*

Communication with the dead was forbidden in Israelite law—and not just by Saul's decree. That makes it surprising that Samuel appears when summoned by this outlaw medium (who seemed shocked that he actually showed up). Yet this story, along with the appearance of Moses and Elijah on the Mount of Transfiguration, affirms that death is not the end for servants of God.

Message Received

Despite our desire for detailed messages about the nature of life and death and everything else, we tend to get bits and pieces. People return with minds blown, lives changed, but the script is sketchy.

There's one good reason for that: language is overrated.

"Communication in near-death experiences—including the conveying of important messages—is almost always non-physical," according to Dr. Jeffrey Long, author of *God and the Afterlife: The Groundbreaking New Evidence for God and Near-Death Experience*. "The closest phrase in the English language is 'telepathic communication,' but it generally goes beyond that."[2]

NDE pioneer Raymond Moody observed the same phenomenon as people discussed their interactions with heavenly beings: "People claim that they did not hear any physical voice or sounds coming from the being through audible sounds. Rather, it is reported that direct, unimpeded transfer of thoughts takes place, and in such a clear way that there is no possibility whatsoever either of misunderstanding or of lying to the light."[3]

And then there's the translation issue. Moody continues: "This unimpeded exchange does not even take place in the native language of the person. Yet, he understands perfectly and is instantaneously aware."[4] And yet, upon returning, the person needs to put those messages into human language. If you've ever studied a foreign language in depth, you know some phrases are nearly impossible to translate. How much greater the problem must be when the content of the conversation comes from an entirely different mode of being.

Moody quotes one woman who spoke in terms of dimensions. Our world has three. *That* world has more. "And that's why it's so hard to tell you this. I have to describe it to you in words that are three-dimensional. That's as close as I can get to it, but it's not really adequate. I can't really give you a complete picture."[5]

That's why NDE reports are full of *in*direct quotes and sensations. "He said something about this." "I felt she wanted to show me that." "I became aware of something." It might seem that the NDE returnee is being evasive, but it might just be the difficulty of cross-dimensional communication.

The Messages that Get Through

Despite the translation issues, there are still certain messages that come up regularly in reports of those returning from NDEs.

Whether these were heard directly in NDE encounters, sensed indirectly, or just felt in the aftermath, they form a fascinating collection of "heavenly" communication.

God Is Love

People describe being overwhelmed by divine love during these experiences. They feel they are in the presence of love like they've never known. The entire place seems paved with love—fields of flowers growing in the soil of love.

Of course the Bible presents the same message in both poetic and expository terms. God is love (1 John 4:16). And, while you might be familiar with Romans 8:38-39, try rereading it in light of what we're learning about NDEs: "And I am convinced that nothing can ever separate us from God's love. Neither death nor life, neither angels nor demons, neither our fears for today nor our worries about tomorrow—not even the powers of hell can separate us from God's love. No power in the sky above or in the earth below—indeed, nothing in all creation will ever be able to separate us from the love of God that is revealed in Christ Jesus our Lord." (NLT)

> *People describe being overwhelmed by divine love during near-death experiences.*

You Are My Beloved Child

Love does not remain merely a lofty concept; it gets personal. People feel loved, embraced, welcomed. *In spite of the fact that they may go through a "life review,"* NDE returnees say they feel utter acceptance, rather than shame, over bad decisions they've made.

In 2009 Jim Bay suffered a serious fall and was in a coma. As he wrote later, he saw another man with "a kind, weathered face and a long beard. He wore a robe. . . . The air around him sparkled with iridescence. . . . And I knew without a doubt. I was staring into the face of God."

Though Jim was ready for death, he sensed God saying, "It's not your time, Jim. There are things left for you to do for me."

Jim couldn't believe there was much that he could do for God. "I'm no one special," he protested. "I don't go to church. I don't even read the Bible!"

"You are special because you are my child. You don't have to know the Bible to know me. My blessing is in everything. Learn to see those blessings and treasure them. Then tell everyone about me . . ."[6]

Do You Love Me?

Raymond Moody reports that one result of the nonverbal messages of NDEs is that many "try to formulate the thought into a question."[7] That is, they felt they weren't being given information but being asked about their own readiness for death. One man, describing an encounter with "a light of perfect understanding and perfect love," mentally sensed the question, "Lovest thou me?"[8]

That phrasing is from the King James Version of John 21:15-17, in Jesus's post-resurrection interview with Peter. Many believe that by asking this question three times, Jesus was reminding Peter of his threefold denial—and forgiving him for it.

This question then becomes a natural completion of a cycle of relationship. God is love in an overarching way, God loves you individually, now do you love God? If so, then that love could be realized in one of two ways—stay here and enjoy the presence of God, or return to earth and serve God there.

When Peter told Jesus that he did, in fact, love him, Jesus gave him work to do, leading the flock of believers. Many NDE reports include a similar message: *There's more work to do on earth.*

You Have to Go Back

After a kayaking accident, Mary C. Neal was near death. She felt embraced by Jesus and led through beautiful surroundings by a group of robed "beings." But then there was a point of decision. The leader of that robed group told her there was more for her to do on earth. She had to return.

"I had absolutely no intention of coming back," she says now, acknowledging that she had a great family, a great job, a great life on earth. It was just that this place she'd been transported to was amazing. "I felt like I was absolutely *home.*"[9]

Some people report making that choice themselves, but many get the message "It's not your time yet." In some cases, they're given specific tasks.

Elisabeth Kübler-Ross, another pioneer in the study of death and dying, writes about her youngest patient, a two-year-old boy named Peter. An allergic reaction to medication put him at death's door. When he came back to consciousness, he said he had been with Jesus and Mary. It was Mary who told him, "You have to get back, Peter. You have to save your Mommy from the fire."

Relating the story, the boy said, "You know, Mommy, when she told me that I ran all the way back home."

The mother assumed that this was a reference to hellfire, but she was already a woman of great faith, so this confused and bothered her. But in counseling with Kübler-Ross many years later, Peter's mother realized that her life would have been hellish without her dear boy. This was surely the "fire" Mary was talking about—in a clear metaphor the child would respond to.[10]

I Am with You Always

Four-year-old Alma, strangled nearly to death by a drunken relative, had an out-of-body experience in which she sensed the presence of a tall, muscular protector who promised to stay with her. Afterward, she had difficulty talking about her experience. She wasn't talking much at all. But then she sensed this same presence again; she knew from church that this muscular protector was Jesus. "I am with you," she felt him saying. "I have always been with you and will always be with you."[11]

Most NDE reports include a sense of the presence of God's love and light while *there*, but for many it goes much further. As they find themselves back in their bodies, they are more aware of the presence of God than ever before. They remain wrapped in His love, and they may feel called to show His love to others. God becomes an essential part of their lives.

This message—"I am with you always"—matches what Jesus told his followers before He ascended to heaven. (Matthew 28:20) Scripture is full of reminders of God's presence: "Don't be afraid, for I am with you," the Lord promised through Isaiah. "I will strengthen you and help you." (Isaiah 41:10, NLT)

And who can forget the promise of the Twenty-Third Psalm? "Yea, though I walk through the valley of the shadow of death, I will fear no evil: for thou art with me." (Psalm 23:4, KJV) Some have described the NDE passageway as a "valley." In fact, you might consider it, almost literally, as a "valley of the shadow of death." Yet the presence of God fills that space, and He offers to fill our lives on earth as well.

Living in the Wake of Death

What happens as those messages are received and processed? How do people's lives change after an NDE?

The following observations do not hold true for everyone, but for many there is a new pattern of life characterized by freedom and direction. Let's consider some of the results of NDE messages.

Living without the Fear of Death

NDEs demonstrate that death is a journey to a different kind of life, filled with the love and light of our Creator.

> *For many there is a new pattern of life characterized by freedom and direction.*

"When I was a little boy I used to dread dying," says one man interviewed by Raymond Moody. "I used to wake up at night crying and having a fit. . . . But since this experience, I don't fear death. Those feelings vanished. . . . I believe that the Lord may have sent this experience to me because of the way I felt about death. Of course, my parents comforted me, but my parents *showed* me."[12]

Living with Purpose

Nearly every NDE story in this chapter ends with somebody sent back to earth on a mission. There are families to care for, friends to support, causes to champion, ideas to proclaim. For the person returning from an NDE, this is why he or she is back. Life isn't a hobby anymore. There is important, God-ordained work to do.

On her website, Trish Barker extends this sense of purpose beyond the NDE community: "The last part of my NDE showed me that I needed to return to earth and teach. You do not have to be a teacher to live a purposeful life. You do not have to have an NDE to know your life purpose. You only need to infuse your actions with goodness and blessings for others with whatever it is you do in this world."[13]

Living in Love

Mary C. Neal talks about the robes of those guiding her through her NDE as "woven together with fibers of love." It was the same for the building she passed. Love was the mortar that held its blocks together. She knows that sounds strange, but that was what she sensed.[14]

It might not be all that strange, though. The New Testament tells us, "Above all, clothe yourselves with love, which binds us all together in perfect harmony." (Colossians 3:14, NLT) In fact, the language of love pulsates through the Scriptures. Again and again, as people wonder what's most important, the Bible answers, "Love" (for example, Matthew 22:37-39; John 13:34-35; 1 Corinthians 13:13).

People often come back from an NDE with an overwhelming sense of God's love. It only makes sense that they would feel compelled to share it.

Living in Grace

One of the most curious parts of a near-death experience is the life review. You might expect that this would sour the whole experience. Even the best of us have bad spots in our lives, selfish choices, hurtful acts, actions we feel ashamed of. So you might anticipate a major scolding, if not out-and-out rejection. But that's not the testimony of most people who have had an NDE.

> *One of the most curious parts of a near-death experience is the life review.*

"They found, much to their amazement," writes Raymond Moody, "that even when their most apparently awful and sinful deeds were made manifest before the being of light, the being responded not with anger and rage, but rather only with understanding, and even with humor." One woman said, "His attitude . . . was just that I had been learning, even then."[15]

Mary C. Neal had a similar experience in her life review: "It had absolutely nothing to do with judgment. It had everything to do with God's unimaginable love and grace."[16]

Does this casual attitude to the life review mean that right and wrong don't matter?

Perhaps it shows the power of grace.

The Lord is compassionate and merciful,
  slow to get angry and filled with unfailing love.

He will not constantly accuse us,
  nor remain angry forever.
He does not punish us for all our sins;
  he does not deal harshly with us, as we deserve.

The LORD is like a father to his children,
  tender and compassionate to those who fear him.
For he knows how weak we are;
  he remembers we are only dust. (Psalm 103:8-10, 13-14, NLT)

Those who return from NDEs, having experienced such a compassionate life review, say they are driven by the love of God: forgiveness, understanding, second chances.

Living with Appreciation

It's hard to take life for granted when you've nearly lost it. Those who are back from NDEs report a greater appreciation for life, especially in its simpler blessings.

"Life, what a beautiful and precious gift!" one wrote. "Why do we take it for granted? I know I did before my accident but not anymore. Each day is beautiful and exciting because I am alive to enjoy

> *Those who are back from NDEs report a greater appreciation for life.*

it. I love the sunrise, the sunset. I watch the birds as they come to the feeder. I watch the little ants as they carry home their loads. I take each day as it comes. I don't live by hours and minutes or seconds anymore. Just day and night, and I am grateful for each new day."[17]

1 Raymond Moody, *Life After Life* (HarperOne, 2015, originally published 1975), 82.

2 Diana Aydin, "5 Messages Received in Heaven," Guideposts, July 23, 2019, https://www.guideposts.org/inspiration/miracles/gods-grace/5-messages-received-in-heaven.

3 Moody, *Life After Life*, 53.

4 Moody, *Life After Life*, 53.

5 Moody, *Life After Life*, 16–17.

6 Jim "Bubba" Bay, " Bubba's Miraculous Encounter with God," Guideposts, Sept. 17, 2018, https://www.guideposts.org/inspiration/miracles/gods-grace/bubbas-miraculous-encounter-with-god.

7 Moody, *Life After Life*, 53.

8 Moody, *Life After Life*, 56.

9 Dr. Mary C. Neal, "Dr. Mary C. Neal Recalls Her Inspiring Near-Death Experience," video, https://www.guideposts.org/inspiration/life-after-death/dr-mary-c-neal-recalls-her-inspiring-near-death-experience.

10 Elisabeth Kübler-Ross, *On Life After Death* (Berkeley, CA: Celestial Arts, 2008, originally published 1991), 59–60.

11 Evan Miller, "The Near-Death Experiences of Children," Guideposts, Jan. 15, 2019, https://www.guideposts.org/inspiration/miracles/gods-grace/the-near-death-experiences-of-children.

12 Moody, *Life After Life*, 91–92.

13 Tricia Barker, "Messages from My NDE," Jan. 25, 2017, https://triciabarkernde.com/tag/messages-from-heaven-nde.

14 Neal, https://guideposts.org/inspiration/life-after-death/
dr-mary-c-neal-recalls-her-inspiring-near-death-experience.

15 Moody, *Life After Life*, 95.

16 Neal, https://guideposts.org/inspiration/life-after-death/
dr-mary-c-neal-recalls-her-inspiring-near-death-experience.

17 Craig R. Lundahl, PhD, "Lessons From Near-Death Experiences
for Humanity," Western New Mexico University, *Journal of Near-
Death Studies*, 12(1) Fall 1993, Human Sciences Press, Inc. Lundahl
is citing Lee Nelson, *Beyond the Veil Volume 1* (Orem, UT: Cedar Fort,
2011), 131.

Keeping the Faith

By Tim Varney, as told to Anita K. Palmer

*As your faith is strengthened you will find that there
is no longer the need to have a sense of control, that
things will flow as they will, and that you will flow
with them, to your great delight and benefit.*

Emmanuel Teney

Jarrod was squeezing me from behind. My seven-year-old stepson
and I were on his aunt and uncle's four-wheeler ATV on our way
to the creek, about a hundred yards from their house. We had just
finished a big family lunch on the hot summer Saturday. Now Jarrod and
I were bouncing on the washboard trail and laughing with every bump.

My brother- and sister-in-law lived on about four acres near the little
town of Garrison, Kentucky, on the Ohio border. I was twenty-nine and
worked as a mechanic. Jarrod and his mother—my wife, Dana—and I
lived just outside town.

"Faster, Dad! Go faster!" Jarrod yelled.

I loved this little kid. I had been glad to become his stepfather when
I married Dana in 1992, almost two years before. His birth father was
occasionally in his life. But Jarrod and I lived together day in and day

out, and I'd always look for chances to hang out, maybe take him fishing and swimming. My two older sons from previous marriages, Andrew and Derric, would join us whenever they visited from Ohio on school breaks and holidays.

Even though we didn't ride the four-wheeler often, I felt confident driving it. We weren't wearing helmets, but no one did around here. In fact, Dana and I didn't even give it a thought, since Jarrod and I weren't going to go very far or fast.

On the edge of the field, the trail cut through the tall grass and bushes and began to angle down toward the water. Kinniconick Creek, which flows into the Ohio River at the state line, can seem like a full-on river in places. I'd guess its widest spot might be ten yards across. Most of the time the water level—especially in the summer—barely reaches my knees, but sometimes you could find a spot deep enough for a swimming hole. If it was shaded by trees and shrubs, all the better.

The track veered to the right as it descended the slope. Then I saw that it was going to zigzag to the left. I'm generally a really cautious guy, but I was going a little too fast for that turn, so I cut the gas and tapped the brakes. My brother-in-law and I decided later that there must have been something wrong with those brakes because it felt like a giant hand grabbed one side of the ATV and gave a huge jerk.

The next thing I remember is standing on the hillside looking down at the crumpled four-wheeler flipped upside down, its wheels spinning. I would later learn that Jarrod had been tossed more than fifteen feet down the hill and, thankfully, had landed in soft dirt without a scratch.

But underneath that ATV was a body. Mine.

Taken to the Gates of Heaven

I remember feeling no concern at seeing myself facedown in the dirt under that machine. I felt no anxiety or even interest. I was much more captivated by what I was seeing across the creek. Coming toward me were two glittering, golden lights. Somehow I knew that whatever they were, they were happy.

It's so hard to describe them. The only thing I can think to use as an example, even if it's kind of strange, is jellyfish. You know how jellyfish float and swirl? How they're gauzelike and light passes through them? That's a little like what these light-beings were like at first—floating, flowing, with what looked like gold glitter glowing inside them.

I couldn't fathom what they were but I was mesmerized. I wasn't frightened. They kept getting closer. Then they came right to me, one on either side of me, and they transformed into humanlike beings.

I'm five foot eleven, and I came up to what I would describe as their chests, so I figured they had to be around eight feet tall. I know I had to look way up to see their faces, which were humanlike. Their features looked male to me, though they had no facial hair. Their skin was fair, similar to mine (I'm Caucasian) but a little darker. They both had hair that was cut in a Dutch boy style. One had straight platinum-blond hair; the other had yellowish hair with a bit of a wave to it. They wore what seemed like white robes.

I never felt any fear at all during the entire episode. I was simply in awe. There was no talking, no voices, no "mental telepathy" or whatever you might call it. I just could feel what they were feeling toward me—an intense feeling of unconditional love.

Then, in a blink of an eye, we went straight up. Immediately we were in another place. The only way I can describe it is as a rolling field full of colorful landscapes that radiated. I remember thinking that the colors were brighter than anything I had ever seen. It felt like the beautiful plants and grass were talking, that they were animated or alive. It felt like it was a place full of such joy that even the plants were happy.

I saw a pathway. I don't remember being aware of my body or of intentionally moving, but I sensed that we were in motion. We were heading to a white city surrounded by a tall white wall. It looked like a physical place, not a mirage. There were domed buildings on the other side of the wall, but I couldn't see more than that.

It felt like the beautiful plants and grass were talking, that they were animated or alive.

When we reached the wall, I felt like I was standing at the bottom of a skyscraper, looking up. That's how tall the wall was. The mental picture in my memory makes me think it was made of something like stone. The two light-beings guided me to a white stone-like bench. They didn't ever use voices as we know them, but I clearly understood that I needed to sit down and stay there for a bit.

I wanted so badly to go into the city. I felt like it was calling to me. I felt an intense yearning.

The pair moved away from me and approached another being, a very tall, slender, male-like figure who was very different from them. From a distance he appeared to have short, dark hair and to be wearing some sort of one-piece garment. It wasn't a robe, but it was black, which was so odd in this beautiful place of pure white. I don't have any idea what or who the being was. I didn't interact with it.

I wished the figure in black hadn't been involved, though, because the two light-beings came back to me and communicated that I was not allowed to enter the city. I had to go back. I knew that meant back to earthly life. They didn't indicate why. I got the sense there was something I had to do, but they didn't say. I remember being overcome with sadness that I couldn't go inside the wall. I really, really wanted to.

I somehow communicated the question, *Will I be able to come back at some point?* I discerned that their answer was yes. They were very gentle and loving with me, but firm.

Then I felt like I was falling, very rapidly, going down a pipe. Glancing back, I could see heaven behind me as though it were a circular hole; the image got smaller and smaller. Then, *thump!* I was back in my body.

A Message of Hope

If you met me on the street, you wouldn't give me a second glance. I'm just an average guy, born and raised in southern Ohio. I'm a mechanic and a truck driver. (Or I was. I'll get to that later.) I'm a dad and brother. I was a son but my parents are dead now. I've made a lot of mistakes and I've done a bunch of stupid things, but I've tried to live by the Golden Rule and follow Christ.

I was married twice before Dana. When my girlfriend, Angela, and I were seniors in high school, she discovered she was pregnant. We got married as soon as we graduated and I went right to work to support my family. My son Andrew arrived in 1983. He is now a nurse practitioner and lives about ten miles from me.

Unfortunately, the marriage didn't work out and Angela and I divorced not long after we were married. Eventually I tied the knot again, this time to Debbie. We were together for about seven years, and our son Derric was born in 1986. He also lives near me now, and has two wonderful daughters, my granddaughters. Debbie and I divorced in 1992.

I had two broken marriages before I was twenty-seven—not something I was proud of.

"God's Gonna Do Something Wonderful with You"

As I gained consciousness after the ATV accident, I felt my face pressed into the dirt and the weight of the machine on my back. My brave little stepson was grabbing at it and trying to move it.

"Dad! Dad! I'll get it off you! I'll get it off you!"

It didn't budge. I remember being able to lift my head enough to tell Jarrod to stand back. I don't know if it was from a rush of adrenaline or if I had supernatural help, but I raised my back and tossed the four-wheeler off me. It wasn't a small ATV either. I watched it somersault a few times down the hill before landing on its wheels, rocking like a toy.

Then I sort of sat, sort of collapsed in the grass and rocks. I was dazed and rattled. Actually, I was really banged up. I didn't have any broken bones, but my body was scraped and bruised and missing skin. My clothes were shredded in places.

I felt numb but I did manage to ask Jarrod if he was all right. "Yeah! I'm fine, Dad," he said. He looked up.

Dana, my sister-in-law, and brother-in-law were at the top of the hill, about a hundred yards away, staring down. Still to this day, I don't know how they knew they needed to check on us. I can't imagine they could have heard the crash from back at the house—Jarrod and I were below the level of the fields. We never talked about it, but I still wonder how they got to us so quickly, and now we've lost touch.

"Jarrod, are you all right?" Dana yelled as the three of them started scrambling down the trail. "Tim! Are you okay?"

When they reached us, Dana hugged Jarrod as she looked at me, a question on her face. *What the heck happened?* I couldn't answer that. But I told her what I did know.

"I saw an angel," I said.

"What?!" she said. My sister- and brother-in-law froze and listened too.

How do you describe something that's more real than reality? How do you paint a picture of the afterlife?

"An angel. Two of them actually." Then I shared a little of what had happened. Or I tried to. How do you describe something that's more real than reality? How do you paint a picture of the afterlife?

My brother-in-law helped me climb back up the hill, and we all walked slowly through the dry, hot fields to the house. Nobody said much. Dana got me out of my torn clothing and into a shower to begin cleaning up my wounds. Then I lay down and she doctored me up.

I could hardly walk for a few days, which gave me a lot of time to think about what had happened.

The pastor of Dana's church came to visit. She was an older lady, real quiet. I liked her. Dana and her extended family attended the church, and I often went too.

"I heard ya got t'see some things," the pastor said, looking intently at my face.

Everyone said this preacher lady was able to discern things about people—as if she had extrasensory perception or something. She wasn't real healthy. I heard she had a history of ministrokes. Maybe she herself had had a near-death experience or something like it.

"Yeah," I said. "I mean, I don't know, really, what I saw, but . . ." I went on to describe some of what happened. She listened. I expected her to tell me I probably just had a hallucination or something, to open up her Bible and try to prove to me that I couldn't have seen what I saw. But she didn't even follow up with questions.

She just smiled. "That's good. God's gonna do something wonderful with you."

The First NDE

My near-death experience after the four-wheeler accident wasn't my first. Something odd happened to me when I was seventeen. It had been so confusing that I stuffed the memory deep into the back of my adolescent mind—so deep that I didn't even think of it at the time of the four-wheeler incident. But looking back now, I know there definitely was a connection.

> *Something odd happened to me when I was seventeen. I stuffed the memory deep into the back of my mind.*

I had just had my wisdom teeth pulled. I was at home, in the little town of Waverly, Ohio, where I was raised with my sister and four brothers. I was lying on the couch, resting. No one else was around. My mouth was packed with cotton, but I was feeling pretty good. Not groggy or anything. I remember getting up and walking into the bathroom.

The next thing I can recall was hearing two loud thuds. That was me hitting the bathroom sink and the floor.

As quickly as that happened, I found myself in a place that was full of light. I know that's pretty vague, but it's all I can remember. That and the people, or beings that looked like people. They were wearing robes. They were taking care of me, and I knew they loved me very much. I felt an overwhelming feeling of love there.

I don't know how long this experience went on, but I got a sense that I had to return to this world because there was something I had to do. The beings didn't say anything; there was no communication, actually, but my senses were heightened to this thought. I wish I could remember more but that's all of it.

The next thing I knew, my parents were breaking open the bathroom door. My mother told me later that she and my dad found me white and unresponsive, and she thought I was dead. They were frightened! I came to, but somewhat unwillingly. I didn't want to lose that incredible feeling of love.

At the time, I didn't understand this experience, and I didn't mention it to anyone. I had no idea how to deal with a visit by beings in robes and with feeling an overwhelming sense of love. I thought of these beings as heavenly, even though up until then I hadn't given heaven much thought. I eventually came to understand I had had an NDE, but at the time, I didn't know what it was.

A Moral Foundation

My father, Richard, was a smart, quiet man. He worked hard to provide for his family and because of that, it seemed to us kids that he was gone all the time, working long double shifts. My mother, Barbara, stayed home and did most of the parenting of my siblings and me.

While neither of my parents was highly educated, they had high moral standards. I know they believed in Jesus and the Bible even though we didn't practice religion much at home. When they mentioned God or Jesus or spiritual matters, it was always with respect. But for some reason—I never asked why—regular church attendance and

> *It took a long while for me to trust Jesus completely with my life.*

talk about living a life with Jesus wasn't part of our family.

However, my twin brother, Patrick, and I sometimes went to Sunday school on our own. Pat and I would walk to the church, which was only a few blocks from our house. Or sometimes we would ride the little Sunday school bus that the church sent around the neighborhood. Any kid with their folks' permission could jump on. That was fun.

Mom encouraged Pat and me to attend church. We were the youngest of the six; I guess the older four were not interested. Looking back, I think Mom would have liked to go to church with us. I don't know what kept her from it.

Even with my early interest, it took a long while for me to trust Jesus completely with my life. While I have always tried to live a Christian life, I didn't feel close to Christ—until I encountered Him in a deeper way after I had my third near-death experience.

Close to Death

My third and fourth NDEs are intertwined with my health issues, so I need to share some medical details in order to talk about my experiences with life on the other side of the veil.

My health problems started in 1999 without warning and with a terrible bang. I was thirty-four. I was in great shape, 195 pounds, solid muscle. I could run all day. With the work I was doing, I had to be tough. I was a commercial truck driver for a waste-removal company.

The company base was in Circleville, Ohio, an hour and a half north of where Dana, Jarrod, and I were living in Kentucky. Oftentimes I would have to cover another driver's route, which meant I would be working a pretty brutal sixteen-hour day. I'd have to get up in the wee hours, drive that hour and a half from Garrison to base to pick up my rig, and then spend the day on my route. The job wasn't just sitting in the cab either; I was in and out, shoving dumpsters around and yanking receptacles. Sometimes I'd be so exhausted at the end of my shift that I'd sleep in my truck rather than drive back to Kentucky.

On top of the physical demands of my job and the lack of sleep, I was struggling in my marriage to Dana. We hadn't given up, but things were very stressful.

One day I was heading back to base. It was evening and still hot. The July heat that day had reached the upper nineties, if not above one hundred, and the humidity was thick. My route had taken me north of Columbus, Ohio, so I had an hour-and-a-half drive just to turn in my truck at base, then another hour-and-a-half leg home. I stopped at a convenience store to pick up something cold to drink.

I was sucking on a cherry slushy for a few miles when my chest started to hurt. I wondered if I could be having a heart attack, but attributed the pain to the icy beverage hitting my overheated body. I even joked about it with my CB (citizen's band) radio buddies. "Hey. Anybody know what a heart attack feels like? I may be having one." I laughed.

The tightness went away and I finally got home around ten that night and went straight to bed. After a few hours' sleep, I got up to start the next day's work. I didn't feel right but figured I was just sleep deprived. I knew I had to hurry if I wanted to clock in on time. This day I was assigned to a "country route," which was about three hundred miles of rural roads.

As I was getting dressed in the bathroom, my heart started to race so badly I had to lie down. I couldn't make it back to the master bedroom so I dropped instead onto my stepson's bottom bunk bed. I started panting. There was no pain at first. Just breathlessness. I couldn't get any oxygen.

Then it was like my chest was being squeezed by a giant vise. I felt like I was suffocating. Sweat poured out of me as I writhed in pain.

My cries woke Dana and she came running. I couldn't speak. She punched 911 into her phone. The dispatcher assured her paramedics would arrive soon. Then she ran across the road to where her parents lived and woke them up, asking them to come stay with Jarrod, who, thankfully, slept through the whole incident. I remember lying there in the dim light, curled into a fetal position, clutching my chest, praying silently. *"Lord! I'm not ready to die. I'm only thirty-four. Please! Don't let me die!"*

After the Damage

We lived out in the boonies, so it took a while for the emergency squad to reach us. The nearest hospital was thirty miles away, across the river in Ohio. I was well aware of the route. I knew the ambulance crew would have to go out of their way to find a bridge and then backtrack to the hospital. And I knew the clock was ticking. It was hard to stay awake because I wasn't getting much oxygen, but something told me if I became unconscious I would never wake up.

I don't remember much about the trip to the hospital. As I lay on a stretcher in excruciating pain I heard the emergency room doctors say that all they could do for me was administer what's known as a clot-buster. By then, my mother, sister, and twin brother had raced down from Waverly. The clot-buster seemed to have no effect, so I was flown by helicopter north to Riverside Memorial Hospital in Columbus.

When the ER staff at Riverside got to me, five hours had gone by since the chest pain started. They did an angioplasty to open up a clogged artery and insert a stint. But the damage had been done. It was bad. I don't remember how many days I spent in the hospital, but while I was flat on my back in the hospital bed, the doctors talked to my wife and my mom. They said that my heart had been so injured by the myocardial infarction—or MI, as the doctors called heart attacks—that if I lasted another fifteen years I'd be a lucky man.

I didn't want to leave the people I loved. But I also was certain there was a better place waiting for me.

When Dana and Mom told me that, I did the figuring in my head. If I stayed alive until I was forty-nine, I'd be able to see my sons reach adulthood. I didn't want to leave the people I loved. But I also was certain there was a better place waiting for me. Not just a hope; I knew that for a fact. There was no doubt in my mind. Then or now.

In addition to that, one of the strongest truths I had come away with during my second NDE was a conviction that we are never actually separated from the people we love. Maybe we're temporarily apart in the physical realm but it's not forever. Here or there, there is only one life. Plus—I don't really know the right way to put it into words—I'm convinced that even if you've left this dimension, you're still connected with the people you love somehow.

In the meantime, though, I had an earthly reality to face. I had to provide for my family. After a couple of months at home recovering, I had to go back to work. I had no choice. I had no savings, and without the job I had no income and no health insurance. I also was pretty stubborn. I clung to my sense of pride, telling myself and anyone else who would listen that I was so tough that this heart issue couldn't kill me. Plus, the crews I worked with were rough. You couldn't show any weakness.

At night I would whisper, "God, please don't let me die."

My cardiologist strongly recommended that I have a pacemaker inserted. I felt like I'd be some kind of machine. He also kept telling me to forget about working, to take it easy and go on disability. "I can't do that. I'm only thirty-four years old," I said.

While my work conditions were much the same—in other words, long, physically demanding days on the road—Dana and I made a few changes. We moved back up to Waverly to be closer to base. That also put me closer to my sons, who spent every other weekend with us.

But the truth was, I was not the same person. Not physically, not emotionally. I was scared. At night I would whisper, "God, please don't let me die."

A Bright Spot among Difficulty

Simultaneous to but unrelated to the crisis with my heart, I started to develop some sort of neuromuscular pain all over, especially in my hips, shoulders, and neck. It got so bad I couldn't even raise my hands up above my head to comb my hair. I finally went to a doctor. He sent me to the Ohio State University Medical Center to see if I could get some answers. The doctors there tested for a range of auto-immune disorders, which are really hard to diagnose. By elimination they came to the conclusion I probably had fibromyalgia. It wouldn't be the last of my diagnoses.

Right about that time, my company was taken over by another outfit. The labor laws had changed concerning the amount of hours allowed for the type of driving I was doing. The new company complied by reducing my driving hours—but not my workload. I was already being asked to do the impossible; now I had to do it in less time.

I finally had to tell my bosses I could not physically do my job because of my bad heart and the fibromyalgia pain and fatigue. So I was taken off the waste-management trucks and put on a front loader. I didn't have to get out and shove dumpsters around, but driving that big truck through cities and suburbs is pretty stressful because it's hard to maneuver through traffic. It wasn't fun.

One bright spot was the birth of my daughter, Makenzie. Dana and I had been together for a decade and she hadn't gotten pregnant, so we thought having a child together wasn't meant to be. We had stopped hoping for it.

When I heard the news, I was shocked. I had figured I would be able to live long enough to see my sons reach adulthood, but I wondered if I'd last long enough to see this baby reach adulthood too. Given what the doctors said about my life expectancy, I wouldn't have chosen to bring a child into the world if I thought I might not be around to help her grow up.

Then I started to think about it. My marriage to Dana was shaky. Maybe raising a daughter together would strengthen the bond. It did, for a while anyway. Sometimes the things that you think won't be good can turn out to be just what you need. Being the father of a daughter has been wonderful, and I ended up having a lot more time with her during her childhood than I was able to with my boys because of what happened with my health. I loved it. Makenzie gave me a lot of joy. She still does.

A Call to the Altar

I can't recall just when it was during this period, but my sister Cindy's church was holding a weeklong revival. It was a small congregation just outside Waverly. She kept inviting me to go with her and I kept thinking *been there, done that.* Back when I lived in Kentucky, I was attending the church Dana's family belonged to and trying to follow Christ as best I could. Looking back, I didn't really have a personal relationship with Him yet. I was committed to Christ. I'll never not be a Christian, no matter what. But I didn't feel like I fit in, really.

Finally, I gave in just to stop Cindy from asking. That night, as the evangelist preached, I had an urge to go up to the altar. But I got stubborn. I kept thinking, *If he says this word, I'll go. If he says that word, I'll go.* It's like I was testing God. Kinda silly, really. *God, if this is real, make him say this one word and I'll go.* But the man never did say the magic words and I stayed seated.

The next morning, I got my truck in Circleville and I drove up north of Columbus and Delaware County for my route. I had arrived a bit early. We weren't allowed to start the route before a certain time, so I had to sit at a gas station just outside of town and wait.

I was gazing out the dusty windshield. Early morning sunlight poured through the trees and over the grass and cast a glow on trash in the parking lot. The inside of my cluttered cab kind of radiated. That's when I heard a voice speak to me.

I can't say if the voice was audible or in my spirit, but I do believe it was the voice of the God I was "testing" the night before. It said, "You need to go to church tonight and go to the altar."

> *Early morning sunlight cast a glow on the parking lot. Then I heard a voice speak to me.*

I laughed and frowned at the same time. "I'm not doing that," I said out loud.

The voice repeated the statement. This time, I answered to myself, *I'm not doing that. I've already been there. I'm not doing it.*

This mental communication continued until I realized God was telling me that the only reason I was still alive was because of Him. He also reminded me what it would be like if He hadn't saved me. At that moment I started experiencing slight chest pains and shortness of breath. That sold me!

Okay, okay. I'll do it. Immediately God reminded me of the nitro-glycerin pill I always carried with me. As I swallowed the pill, the voice said, "I'll see you tonight."

That was it. Still tingling and in awe, I got on the road and started work. The day just flew by. But every so often I'd think about going to the revival service that night and hope few people who knew me would be there.

Then Dana called before my shift ended. "Hey, my mom and sister are coming up and they're going to come to revival up here with me," she said.

Now I was in for it.

Experiencing God's Presence

The night came. My sister, my wife, my mother-in-law, my sister-in-law, and some others I knew were there. I sat, dreading the sermon. A different man was preaching, and I don't remember much of what he said. But when he made the call encouraging people to go to the altar, I went. And I felt nothing.

> *I had tasted heaven. I'd felt the overwhelming love of God.*

You have to understand: I had tasted heaven. I'd felt the overwhelming love of God. I had been embraced by the light. When that was taken away from me, I hungered for it. I knew God was real. What I had experienced as real and true wasn't what I've experienced on earth in what we humans call Christianity. I needed to feel something from God while on earth. I wanted to be able to say, "I feel different now."

I went to work the next morning still feeling distressed about the revival. God Himself had told me to get to the altar. I had obeyed, but nothing had happened. In the middle of my route, I pulled my truck over on the side of the highway and stopped. I didn't want to go another mile before dealing with this situation.

"Look, God," I said, "I did everything you wanted me to do. I obeyed you in front of all those people. I really need to feel something. I need

Your presence. I need Your Spirit. I need You." My wounded heart was crying out to God, yearning for Him, searching.

I waited, thinking back to my NDEs. Then something just came over me, a warmth that welled up inside me. My hands went up and I found myself just praising Jesus. I started crying. I could feel God's unconditional love. God had heard me and answered, and I was so grateful.

I sat there for at least half an hour, savoring the emotions, unwilling to let them go, thanking God and loving on Him. This was the personal relationship I had been missing. Then I got back on the road.

That night I went back to the church and told everybody about what happened. There was a lot of "Praise the Lord!" and hugs all around.

A New Health Challenge

I was able to get my heart issues and fibromyalgia under control and then got hit with another serious health problem. It turns out that I have a condition that causes my heart to slow down and almost stop beating, but it's completely unrelated to my damaged heart. The condition has a very long name: vasovagal neurocardiogenic syncope. Most of the time the docs say cardio syncope. Or just syncope, pronounced like sink-o-pee.

Syncope can occur without any trigger or warning, but most of the time it is caused by things like heat exposure, standing for a long time, severe pain, intense fear, or emotional distress. Your heart rate drops suddenly. The blood vessels in your legs dilate, or widen, allowing blood to pool in your legs, which lowers your blood pressure. The two situations—the slowed heart rate and the drop in blood pressure—quickly reduce blood flow to your brain, causing you to lose consciousness. At this point, the result is basically the same as when you faint.

Sometimes syncope is relatively harmless; others experience a more dire version. Apparently, I have the worst version of cardiac syncope. Most of the times I could anticipate it happening and sit down before I fell down. Not always, though. One of my episodes nearly killed me. I have no doubt I was in the midst of one when I experienced my third NDE.

Going over the Edge

It was 2004. I was at base stepping down for the day. I was sorting out my log when I started to lose consciousness. I didn't feel like I was having a heart attack but I wasn't sure. I blacked out. When I came to, I was able to get on the two-way radio. I woke up the dispatcher and told him I needed an ambulance.

I was conscious when the paramedics arrived. They said I was white as a ghost and sweat was pouring out of me. I couldn't catch my breath, which sometimes but not always indicates a heart attack. I was uncomfortable but not having chest pains. They had to lift me out of the cab—I couldn't get myself out. When we reached Berger Hospital in Circleville, I was feeling better, although disoriented and exhausted, and I just wanted to go home. The ER docs weren't having it. They couldn't diagnose me, but with my history, they insisted on sending me up to Riverside Memorial Hospital in Columbus.

At Riverside the doctors said they thought what I had experienced in the truck was an effect of my tachycardia, a racing heart rate I often have. But they wanted to admit me and do a battery of tests. One test I failed in a very big way.

I hadn't heard of a tilt-table test. It's designed to help diagnose unexplained syncope, or dysautonomia, a condition in which the autonomic nervous system doesn't work properly. The goal is to trigger symptoms like light-headedness, dizziness, or actual fainting while your heart rate and blood pressure are being monitored. If that sounds unpleasant, I assure you it is.

I was strapped to a table that looked like a giant gurney. My chest and legs were strapped down with wide bands. Electrode patches on my chest, legs, and arms con-

The sensation was as if I were on top of a skyscraper about to fall.

nected me to an electrocardiogram machine to monitor my heart rate. I was also hooked up to a blood pressure monitor.

The name of the test gives a clue as to what they do to the table once you're tied down. A horizontal platform sticks out at the foot of the table. When the table is elevated to eighty degrees, your feet are lodged as if on a mini ledge, like you're standing on the top of a building with your toes hanging over the edge. In my case, I was also facing a wall-sized photograph about six or eight feet away of multicolored trees that were out of focus.

I had to be upright as if standing for maybe fifteen minutes, which may not sound like a long time but it felt like it was. The sensation was as if I were on top of a skyscraper about to fall. Looking back on it, I'm sure that's part of the test in order to create stress. After a few minutes, a doctor gave me a nitroglycerin pill to put under my tongue to dilate my blood vessels.

At first I was completely calm, thinking this was the stupidest test I had ever had. Then all at once, the classic symptoms broke out: sweat, vertigo, tingling, dimmed vision, weakness, overwhelming nausea. It was awful. I sensed I was going to lose consciousness.

"I'm outta here," I whispered.

And then I was instantly someplace else.

Another Glimpse of Heaven

I remember leaving my body and finding myself in a twisting, turning corridor. It was something like a hallway but with no ceiling. Above me was a beautiful, multicolored light with different-colored rays coming out of it. It was full of love. I don't know how I knew that but I did. All I could think of was reaching that light. I was overwhelmed with the desire to get to it. I remember being excited about it. I wanted to touch the light so badly that I started chasing it, although I don't know how or even if I was moving in the sense we'd understand it here on earth.

Just as I appeared to be gaining on it, I seemed to be lifted up so that I was above the entire area of color. Looking down, I saw a vast labyrinth—a beautiful endless maze as far as I could see. No beings, though. A sense of love, yes, but no message.

In one swift motion, I was sucked back into my body, like a tennis ball in a vacuum hose.

Then in one swift motion I heard a thud as I was sucked back into my body, like a tennis ball in a vacuum hose.

I opened my eyes. I was on my back on the table, now horizontal. A doctor and nurse were leaning over me asking if I was all right. Both looked concerned.

"Yeah, I'm okay." It was a lie, of course. How could I be okay, having to taste the glories of heaven and then leave them behind again? I was consumed with extreme disappointment and sadness.

Of course, I knew the medical people were asking if I was physically okay. Honestly, I didn't know. I had no idea what had just happened. They told me that I'd had a seizure, which is not uncommon with this condition due to the lack of blood flow to the brain. But what was uncommon, they said, was how quickly and instantly I went out. They were shocked. They had worried that my heart had stopped. My blood pressure had dropped dramatically too. They said that my reaction to the test was the worst they had ever seen.

All I could think of at that moment was how much I didn't want to be back here, back on earth. Why hadn't God let me die? I was furious and disappointed.

During the subsequent days in the hospital and then for months afterward, I kept asking God, *Why have you been giving me another taste of the afterlife then forcing me to return to the present?* I just didn't get it. Yes, I remembered what the lady pastor had said years before, about God having plans for me. But it didn't lessen the fury and disenchantment that would follow me through the next few years, a period that would turn out to be the worst of my life.

The Toughest Years

After this incident, my doctors ordered me to stop working. That meant I had to give up my commercial driver's license. Even though I tried to explain that truck driving was my livelihood, there was no discussion. I felt helpless and furious, even though I understood their reasoning. That was the end of that.

The government declined my application for disability, even with the medical records and physicians' statements. It wasn't too long before we couldn't make payments on the modular we had set up outside Waverly. Dana found work here and there, but it wasn't enough. Within a year our home was repossessed.

Through it all I kept praying, "God, what am I going to do about this?" The answer that kept popping into my head was: *Do nothing.*

I loved my family, but I could not shake the yearning for the ultimate reality I had tasted.

Because that thought was one that was absolutely counter to my nature, I had to accept that it was from God.

Doing nothing is not really my strong suit. I had always been proud at being able to work hard and provide, despite all my health challenges. Dana and the kids understood why I had to stop working. It wasn't them who made me feel useless. It was me. What was I good for now? Why was I still here?

My mom loaned us enough to get a small mobile home to live in, and I was grateful, but it was humiliating. On top of being pretty depressed and feeling physically awful, debt collectors were harassing me as if I were a criminal. *What was the point of this, Lord?* I wondered every day.

I was angry, frustrated, and disappointed. I didn't want to be here. I loved my family, but I could not shake the yearning for the ultimate reality I had tasted. This reality was a poor shadow.

It took me four years of fighting to get the disability pay I qualified for. It was four long years of filling out a mountain of paperwork, collecting statements, making appeal after appeal, and working with an attorney. Eventually, the judge at my hearing ruled 100 percent in my favor and ordered retroactive payments. I rejoiced, even though it came too late for us to hold on to our home. One positive: The collection agency was found guilty of unlawful techniques. Because of that, all the negative credit marks on my records were removed.

After the victorious disability ruling, I was able to pay back my mom and rent a house in Waverly a few houses down from my mother's home. It was a happy day when Dana, Makenzie, and I moved in. Because I was closer to my mom, I began looking after her more regularly. Plus, it was nice for Makenzie, who at five loved being around her grandmother. Of course, her grandmother loved it too.

I will say this: Those four years of struggle, trauma, and uncertainty forced me to turn to God to provide. Everything was taken away. Pain and suffering are powerful teachers. My pride got worn down and my faith got strengthened. Not to perfection, of course. But I began to truly trust God. I learned to be satisfied with whatever God had for me. If God said, *Tim, tonight you're going to eat a bologna sandwich for dinner,* I was satisfied with that. Or, if He said, *Here's a car; it's not new and it's got some problems but it's going to get you from here to there,* I was all right with that. I learned to be satisfied with whatever God put in front of me.

Another positive thing that occurred during these really tough years was that I picked up my guitar again. I had been into music as a teenager, playing both in bands and by myself, and working on amplifiers and that sort of thing. I loved country, rock, funk, all kinds of stuff. Working long hours in my twenties and thirties while caring for a family sucked up any time I could have put toward music. Now, music helped to soothe my soul.

Trapped and Tortured

Once we were in our new home, my stress lessened a bit. Things were physically okay with me until I developed some kind of intestinal problems. I had severe abdominal pain on a few occasions that required an emergency room visit. I also found that I had to stay pretty close to the bathroom. The doctors couldn't figure out what was going on, but they found fluid in my abdomen. They never determined how it got there, but one theory was some sort of a perforated bowel.

One morning I got up and I went to use the bathroom and felt severe pain in my abdomen. Then something occurred I don't like to remember—shock bowel. It's almost like you lose all the fluid in your body instantly.

I eventually stumbled back into bed after the first episode and then I had another upset. I hurried back to the bathroom and then I couldn't do anything else because it triggered a syncope episode that would not stop. Nausea, vertigo, blacking out. It was really bad. My syncope episodes are very unpleasant, so having one on top of this intestinal thing was torture. I became trapped in the bathroom, my head between my knees, trying to just stay conscious.

Jarrod was with us at the time, and he and Dana decided they'd better call 911. I don't know if I lost consciousness or not but when the squad finally got there I couldn't talk. They got right down by my ears to talk to me, but I couldn't respond.

They leveraged me onto a narrow wheelchair of some sort and wheeled me out of the bathroom through the hallway into the living room. That's where they had set up their stretcher. Then one of them bent down and said, "Sir, you need to stand up and get to the stretcher." I'm thinking, *I can't, I can't.* I still couldn't speak so I shook my head. They said they'd help. One got on either side of me.

Back then, I had put on some weight from not working and just sitting around, so I was kind of a big guy. On a count of three they pulled me up into a standing position.

That's the moment I found myself somewhere else.

The Fourth NDE

I was not in my living room anymore. Dana, Jarrod, and the EMTs were nowhere to be seen. Instead, I was in an expansive space full of boundless, golden light. I saw no massive white wall like in my second NDE or the labyrinth from my third NDE; the general setting was more like the one in my first NDE. I did, though, feel the same incredible love. The light was love; the love was light. I remember a sense of immense relief. Going from the suffering I just had been experiencing to this endless love was pure bliss.

> Going from the suffering I just had been experiencing to this endless love was pure bliss.

To my right I noticed a group of people. I call them people because they had humanlike shapes. I could make out heads, arms, and legs of individual beings. But they seemed to be made of light—like the light that surrounded me.

I don't know if I said it or if I thought it, but I wondered who they were. At that instant they all turned toward me. I sensed they were surprised I was there. They came forward as a group. The closer they got, the more I could see they were indeed beings with human faces. I thought I might be blinded by the light emanating from them but I wasn't.

> *I suddenly recognized that this person was my paternal grandmother, Agnes.*

Two of them continued closer. I saw details that suggested one was male and the other female. The female was beautiful, with shoulder-length auburn hair, fair skin, and full red lips. She had very intense blue eyes. Piercing eyes. She was wearing a white robe. I don't know how I perceived it, but it was clear to me that she was in charge. Power radiated from her being.

I felt overwhelming love from both of them. They were not only emanating light but immersed in it too. I compare it to a fish living in the water. These beings were living in the light like a fish lives in water. The light was part of their whole being.

We began to communicate with each other. Instantly, I knew all about her and she knew all about me. It felt like I was waking up from amnesia. Then I realized that I was home. I knew everyone and they knew me.

I suddenly recognized that this person was my paternal grandmother, Agnes. I just knew. And then I saw that the other individual was a young version of my father—dark hair instead of gray, vibrant skin instead of wrinkled, and brilliant eyes. He didn't communicate with me at all, but I could feel his love and concern for me.

What I was seeing wasn't so much the grandmother and father I knew on earth but their essence. Let's call them their souls, for lack of a better term, the beings who are eternal.

The woman I recognized as my grandmother conveyed that everything was going to be okay. Right off the bat she told me I wasn't there to stay, that I was only going to be there until the doctors got my body fixed up enough to where I could inhabit it again. The message—not by voice but somehow by consciousness—was, "We're just here to take care of you."

I had no sense of time. I felt flooded by a stream of thoughts, concepts, and mental pictures, but I didn't feel overwhelmed. I got the impression I only had to ask to get information.

The thing I wanted to know most about was Jesus. I never saw Jesus when I was immersed in the love, but it was like He was there, right behind me. I wondered if He had been there. My grandmother and father answered instantly: *He is who He says He is, and He's coming back.*

When? I inquired. *Soon.* I was under the impression that they didn't know exactly when, but they were excited about it.

Then the woman I call my grandmother held her hands up and interlocked her fingers, putting them together like a quarterback does to call for a huddle. I took it to mean everything is going to be united again soon. Earth and heaven will be one.

Then I was told it was time to return. Oh, how I didn't want to go back! This was my happy place. But I had to. The woman reached down. I thought she was going to kiss me. I was pulled away but not before hearing a final message: *Trust in the Lord and pray.* (I took "the Lord" to mean Jesus Christ.)

A Return to Earth

I was sucked back into my body. Jarrod was standing over me, shaking me, hollering "Dad! Dad! Wake up! Wake up!" I was in considerable distress. The EMTs had raised my feet above my head because they had a hard time trying to get a blood pressure reading. My heart rate was 30 beats per minute. (A typical resting heart rate for an adult male is between 60 and 100.) They thought I was dying.

I found out later that my body had collapsed to the floor. My eyes were wide open, my mouth making gurgling sounds. The paramedics tried to lift me onto the stretcher but were struggling. Then Jarrod—who a decade earlier as a young boy had tried to lift the ATV off me—picked me up by himself. He's six foot one and 220 pounds but I was a lot heavier than that. I guess the adrenaline was flowing. It was amazing.

They got me stable to the point where they could transfer me to the local hospital. Dana had called Andrew to meet us there. He could speak the medical language and ask the right questions. I was suffering with the same problems: vomiting, diarrhea, and pain in my abdomen. My blood pressure wouldn't come up. The doctors said they didn't know what else they could do, and I had to be moved to a more advanced facility. Or I would die.

My body had collapsed to the floor. The EMTs thought I was dying.

So they put me in a helicopter and flew me to Riverside Memorial in Columbus. I don't remember the flight or being admitted. The first clear memory was of a nurse in ICU asking me if I knew where I was. Because of all my heart attacks—I think I had had three by then—I had no trouble recognizing Riverside right away.

I spent at least a week there this time. The doctors decided I had probably suffered a perforated bowel, leading to peritonitis. The dehydration and one of my heart medicines may have contributed to the low blood pressure situation. And I'm pretty sure that I had a syncope episode when the EMTs were working on me.

It was a perfect storm I'm glad I haven't had to go through again, even though it led to my fourth NDE.

The Old White Farmhouse

In 2010, I went with my mom and my sister Cindy to Tennessee. They were getting into genealogy and wanted to learn about some ancestors from the eastern part of that state. Makenzie, who was about eight at the time, went with us.

We drove past Knoxville into the Gatlinburg and Pigeon Forge area, close to the Great Smoky Mountains. It was a pretty long drive halfway across the state. We got off the interstate to look around since we hadn't been to this part of the country before. We got lost. We kept looking for signs to get us back to a highway, but the area was really wooded and winding, and we kept getting more confused and frustrated. At one point we just pulled into a dirt driveway to turn around. I glanced a little ways down the drive.

There among leafy trees sat a white farmhouse with clapboard siding, a rusty tin roof, and a sagging porch. It couldn't be! I had seen this house before.

One of the images I was shown during my last NDE was a farmhouse. When I saw it I sensed it was a place I loved, but I didn't recognize it, didn't know who lived there, and didn't know where it was. Yet here it was—the exact scene as the one I had witnessed in my NDE. How could this be? I sucked in my breath and stared. I was astonished.

I kept silent, though. I didn't say, "Cindy! Mom! That's the farm-house from my near-death experience!" They don't know much about my NDEs, and I didn't want to explain right then because they were worried about getting back on the road. Cindy put the engine in reverse and we backed out of there. As we sped away, I turned around to catch the last vision of the farmhouse. I didn't feel the love coming from it that I had during the NDE, but I did feel longing.

What had just happened? And why? Affirmation? It was a mystery. It still is.

"Don't Be Afraid"

Over the next years, because I couldn't work, I helped my mother, was a very involved dad to Makenzie, and had dozens of syncope episodes and six more MIs. Two heart attacks in 2009 led to open-heart bypass surgery and the long difficult recovery it required. In 2011 doctors gave me a new defibrillator/pacemaker. All that intervention didn't prevent two more MIs in 2013. But I kept chugging along, determined to live as long as I could for my daughter.

By the time 2016 rolled around, I'd been taking care of Mom just about full time, with help from Cindy. Mom was still in her home, the same place I grew up in (and eventually bought and am living in now). Her needs were getting worse. She had some dementia and had suffered a stroke and couldn't talk much. I spent as much time with her as possible.

She started to decline pretty fast. Toward the end, I tried to comfort her by sharing a little of my experiences.

"Mom," I said, in the same room my dad died in, "you're getting ready to go someplace wonderful." I described a little of what I had seen, and then said, "Don't be afraid."

Not Yet My Time

During this time when my mom was gravely ill, Dana decided to leave the family. Makenzie and I were devastated. I can't help but think that the stress and sadness may have contributed to another heart attack three months before Mom died.

I was by myself when the heart attack came on. I knew if I called a squad, it would take too long for them to reach me. I had to get to a cath lab as fast as I could. "Cath lab" is the nickname for an examination room in a hospital or clinic where they do cardiac catheterization to visualize the arteries of the heart and the chambers of the heart. It's equipped with diagnostic imaging equipment and staff able to perform coronary angioplasty and coronary stenting and other treatments. At my first MI, the massive one, the little hospital nearest to me didn't have a cath lab, which is why the damage was so major.

I was by myself when the heart attack came on. I could barely breathe. The pain was awful.

I've been through this drill so often that I knew to keep a level head and just go. So, although I could hardly breathe, I drove myself the forty minutes to the hospital in Chillicothe. The pain was awful. I felt like I was being crushed. I wasn't driving like a maniac, though. It would be dumb to be having a full-blown heart attack on your way to the hospital and be killed in an automobile accident.

On the way, I called ahead to the hospital. I told them I was coming and described my route. I said if they did not see me in the next twenty-five minutes to send somebody out to find me. Then I called my nearest son, Derric, who met me at the hospital. Derric has always been there when I needed him—there's probably nothing he wouldn't do for me.

When I walked in, the ER staff was skeptical of my claim. I'm sure they get people coming in all the time saying they're having a heart attack and instead their pain is a result of gas or something. But they hooked me up and saw the EKG. One of them said, "Whoa! You really are having a heart attack!"

> *If God wants me home, then that's where I'll go. I know where I'm going when I die.*

Although this might sound so matter-of-fact, the whole experience was nerve-racking. I could have died en route or had a car accident. The technicians in the cath lab could have applied too much pressure in the balloon they inserted to open up the artery. But I pretty much have the attitude that if God wants to take me, He will. I will do everything I can to stay for Makenzie and my boys, but if God wants me home, then that's where I'll go. I know where I'm going when I die.

Called to Go On

Since the last NDE I've noticed that I seem to know what kind of person a stranger is. I sense their spirit. Sometimes I also get a perception of things that are going to happen in the world. Not detailed visions and not fortune-telling stuff. Just a feeling. For example, when people in this country were just learning about COVID-19, I saw a news clip and got a strong feeling that things were going to turn very serious soon. I wish I hadn't been right.

I have a sense of urgency to encourage people, especially given all that's going on in the world right now. We can't give up on life.

Love, peace, a sense of relief, and extreme joy were common denominators in all my NDEs. It has been hard having those experiences and intense feelings and then having them taken away. Part of me wishes that I didn't remember any of my NDEs. It feels like I'm missing part of me. But I'm not. God is here. And He has called me to simply go on.

I try to put the calling in perspective. I have people who need me and people I love. From time to time, I'm still visited by the presence of the love I experienced in my NDEs. It covers me and consoles me and helps me to continue on my journey. No matter how bad life can get, I have something fabulous to look forward to. I know I'm here for a reason and I'll get to go home when I'm done here.

My Life since My Near-Death Experience

Tim Varney

I have had four near-death experiences, and in all of them, I was given no specific instructions other than to trust in the Lord.

I've always wondered, why me? Why was I chosen to get a glimpse of heaven and then return? I don't have any answers, but one thing I have concluded is that the NDEs somehow were all acts of mercy, because all four occurred when I was in grave medical trouble.

Q *What has been the biggest challenge in returning to an earthly life after your NDEs?*

A The NDEs changed my whole perception of reality. The memories, the feelings, the longing to return to heaven—to go home—never go away. In fact, the NDEs feel more real to me than what we call reality here on earth.

Q *Have you felt unsure of whether or not you should tell people about your NDEs?*

A At times I have been a little uncomfortable sharing my experiences, but at the same time I feel the urge to tell people to help them transition to eternity so they won't be afraid to die.

I hope by sharing my story, readers will know to keep going, to keep the faith. I want people to know that this life on earth, no matter how good or how bad it is, is nothing compared to eternal life. I want to share hope of an afterlife that is wonderful beyond your wildest dreams.

Before my mom died in December 2016 I shared with her some of what I witnessed during my NDEs. I was sad when she died but knew that she was experiencing firsthand the heaven I tried to describe to her.

Q In reliving your NDEs, do you recall aspects of them that at the time didn't make sense but now do?

A In my fourth NDE, among all the images my consciousness was taking in, one stood out, and I don't know why. It was a simple, old white farmhouse, down a tree-lined dirt road. The structure was one story, with a tin roof and a covered wooden porch running the width of the front. I felt that I had some connection to that house, that it was a place I loved.

I puzzled about this image for years afterward but never figured out what and where it was and why I loved it so much. Nor did I understand why it was being shown to me.

I saw the farmhouse in Tennessee when I went there with my mom and sister Cindy. I was shocked. The farmhouse I saw in Tennessee was the exact same farmhouse I saw in my NDE. I still don't know why I was shown the house both times, but seeing it in my human reality reassured me that heaven is real.

Q *What do you want people to learn from you as you share your near-death experiences?*

A I play in a band with some buddies. We like to sing contemporary Christian music. One of my favorite songs is "Temporary Home," sung by Carrie Underwood. She cowrote it with Luke Robert Laird and Zachary David Maloy. The lyrics have great meaning for me, especially the chorus. It captures my thinking about living on earth and anticipating eternity.

> This is my temporary home,
> It's not where I belong
> Windows and rooms
> That I'm passing through
> This is just a stop on the way to where I'm going
> I'm not afraid because I know
> This is my temporary home.

This life on earth is temporary. Heaven is real. It's easy to get caught up in the routines and disappointments of everyday life. I've been through some rough years, but God has shown me that there is something better at the end of my journey here. I can't stop thinking about how God has blessed me, but I also can't wait to go home.

A Divine Message

By Beth Praed, as told to C. Hope Flinchbaugh

Everything in life has purpose. There are no mistakes, no coincidences. All events are blessings given to us to learn from.

Elisabeth Kübler-Ross

My mother pulled the thermometer out of my mouth and held it to the light. Her eyes crinkled up as she studied the red mercury line. She glanced over at my father. "Still over 104," she said, her voice trembling.

Pops, as I affectionately called my father, leaned over my bed. "How do you feel now, Beth? Any better?"

I breathed in to answer him but stopped halfway. *How can breathing stab into my chest like this?* I wondered. *Take little breaths,* I told myself. *Little breaths.*

"Beth?"

I shook my head. "No," I whispered.

Mom put a straw in my mouth. I drank a little water, then pulled back, gasping for air. Pain shot through my chest. Mom handed me two pink baby aspirin, the medical fare recommended for fevers by most doctors in the early 1970s.

"Chew these slowly and swallow," she said gently. "They taste good, like orange candy."

I grimaced. I thought about the boy in the aspirin commercial on television and wondered if he really liked the taste. I nodded and took the two aspirin from her hand.

"Here's a drink for you as soon as you get the aspirin down," she said soothingly.

"Mom?"

"What is it, Beth?" Mom asked. She cupped my chin in her hand.

I worked to catch my breath. "It hurts—to breathe."

My mom looked over at my dad. "Do you think she picked up a virus at her birthday party yesterday?" Pops asked. "Was anyone sick?"

Mom shook her head. "Not that I know of, but I am going to make a few phone calls to their moms just to make sure."

My thoughts flashed back to yesterday, my ninth birthday party. What a blast! At school I was always shy, but yesterday was different, maybe because my party was at my house. I didn't feel shy at all! We lived at the end of a cul-de-sac in suburbia, right outside Indianapolis. Our backyard had a few large trees, a garden with flowers that were just beginning to bud, and a swing set and sandbox where my two younger brothers and I amused ourselves for hours.

My party was so much fun. Mom baked our family favorite "Praed" birthday cake, which is always chocolate with white icing and made only on birthdays. My last name Praed sounds like *prayed*, and my friends thought eating a "prayed" birthday cake was funny. I was thrilled to receive a few Barbie dolls and outfits, but my favorite part of the whole day was running around outside with my friends, playing tag, hide-and-seek, and red light, green light. May is a beautiful time of year in Indianapolis, and we all made the most of its treasures.

But today wasn't fun at all! My mother sponged my face with the cool washcloth one more time and then pulled the pink quilt up to my chin. "You lie here and try to go to sleep," she said as she patted down the sides of the bed. "I'm going to make a few phone calls; I'll be right back."

I closed my eyes and listened to the sound of my breathing—I made such a strange sound. The inside of my ears felt hot. I heard Mom talking on the phone downstairs to the mother of my friend Julie.

I couldn't kneel beside the bed tonight, but praying seemed like a good thing to do.

Julie and I were best friends. She didn't have a dad at home like I did. I remember one time at recess she was crying because she was lonely for her dad. I knew that I was pretty lucky to have two parents at home, and both of them loved me so much.

I heard my mother say goodbye to Julie's mom and hang up the phone. I listened for Mom's footsteps to return to my bedroom so we could pray together before I fell asleep, but she stopped in the hallway. She and Pops were talking in low tones. We always knelt beside my bed and prayed together before I went to sleep at night, but maybe she forgot about bedtime prayers. I knew I couldn't kneel beside the bed anyway, not tonight. I could barely breathe without pain. Still, praying seemed like a good thing to do.

I felt so close to my mother each night when we prayed together. She led my brothers and me in bedtime prayers every night, and she had the whole family attend our small Baptist church each week. Between my mother and our church, I was familiar with prayer, but I really didn't have my own relationship with God. I had never tried to talk to God on my own.

The pain in my chest brought my thoughts back to the present. I wondered about my homework, untouched because of the party yesterday. It was Memorial Day weekend. Would I make it back to school on Tuesday?

I must have fallen asleep because I heard my mother's voice in the distance. "Beth, try to wake up."

Mom?

I shivered.

"Jack, I need more water," she said to my father. "Cool water, not icy."

The weight of the blanket lifted. My head hurt. My chest hurt. Even my skin hurt. Someone put water on my feet, my ankles, my legs.

"No, no, no," I whispered. I had never been in so much pain.

"Ooooo," I breathed. A sharp pain shot through my middle.

"I'm sorry, Honey." Mom's voice sounded funny—high-pitched and strained. "Your father and I are trying to cool you down."

The cold washcloth touched my stomach and I shook uncontrollably.

"No, no, no," I whispered. Each time the washcloth touched me, my skin hurt. I had never been in so much pain. My mother soaked my skin with cool water until it dried and then started all over again. To me, it was agony.

I closed my eyes tight to ward off the pain. The washcloth touched my neck—I shook violently, even on the inside. Mom and Pops were talking, but their voices grew distant . . .

An Unexpected Hospital Stay

I tried to open my eyes, but they refused. So I listened. I heard shuffling and movement and then voices of people who sounded like they were far away. Something hummed near the head of my bed.

At least Mom stopped that awful sponge bath, I thought. The room smelled of alcohol. *I hope she isn't going to rub that all over my body! Mom? Where are you?* I moved to get up. I slid my foot out from under the sheet, but my right arm didn't move. I would find out later that a nurse had inserted an IV into my vein, the hospital's attempt to put fluids back into my dangerously fevered body.

Mom?

Pain seared through my chest. Something was over my face! I used my other arm to reach up and felt a hand cover mine.

"Hi there, Beth," a lady's voice said. "You're in the hospital and you have a special mask on your face to help you breathe. Your mom and dad will be back later. I'm your nurse tonight."

The nurse's voice was kind. Even so, it took some time for me to comprehend her words and my surroundings. She dabbed my forehead with a cool washcloth, and then explained that visiting hours were over and my parents would be back the next morning.

My eyes flew open and I quickly found the only window in the room. It was dark outside! I gripped the stiff hospital sheets at my sides. Would the nurse turn off the lights? Panic rose in my throat. I could endure the sponge bath and the IV needle, but not the darkness! *Please, not the darkness!*

At home, Mom turned on the closet light for me every night. Without the light, I was convinced that ghosts and monsters moved about under my bed. I hated it when they made noises. Sometimes I saw their shadows and that scared me the most. Mom said I imagined it, but the monsters seemed real to me! At least with the light on in my bedroom closet, I knew I wouldn't have to see them—ghosts are scared of the light.

The nurse lifted my hand. "You can let go of the sheet, Beth," she said in a quiet voice. "I've got you."

My hand was all sweaty, but the nurse didn't seem to mind. She pressed her fingers into my wrist and looked at her watch. When she looked up she asked, "Are you thirsty?"

I nodded. The mask over my face kept me from saying—or drinking—anything. The nurse lifted the mask a little and slipped in a straw. The juice tasted wonderful!

"The light," I whispered. Stabbing pain shot through my chest. "Ooo!"

The nurse quickly removed the straw and placed the mask over my face again. "Is that better?"

I nodded. I felt tears on my cheeks. I didn't get to tell her about the light.

"Your mother told me about the light," she said gently. "I was going to leave these side lights on for you all night. Would you like that?"

I nodded. She walked to a door that I guessed was a bathroom. She flipped on the light and propped open the door. I heard the water in the sink running. "I'll leave on the bathroom light too," she called from inside.

Relief washed over me. I wanted to hug that nurse! She returned with a warm washcloth and wiped the tears off my cheeks, just above the mask. The nurse removed the mask briefly, placed the straw in my mouth again, and let me take another sip of the cool juice.

The lights are on, I told myself. *The lights will stay on.*

The machine beside my head hummed a rhythm that seemed to match when my mask filled with air. *Maybe monsters don't like machines that hum at night.* The smell of alcohol faded as I drifted off to sleep.

In and Out of Consciousness

Beth, wake up." My mother's voice sounded far away. Was she touching my arm? Mom called me again.

"Beth, I need to talk to you. Can you hear me?"

I was awake, but I wasn't really awake. It was foggy. *When did my room get this way,* I wondered.

I smelled my dad's cologne. He leaned close so I could feel his warm breath when he whispered in my ear. "I love you, Beth."

I love you, Pops. I don't think he heard me.

I drifted away from them, in spite of

> *I drifted in and out of consciousness for nearly a week. I barely remember being awake.*

my attempts to answer. What did Mom want to talk about?

Later on I found out that I drifted in and out of consciousness for nearly a week. I barely remember being awake, but each time I woke up in the daytime my mom was right there. She always had a cheerful word, but her face, etched with worry, told me her true feelings. Mothers and daughters sometimes have that kind of communication, the kind where no words are needed.

She smoothed back my hair, adjusted my sheets, or read me stories. Once she told me that my friends at school were praying for me. *Who told them to do that?* I wondered. Later I found out that my mom called the school and asked the teachers and students to pray for me. In the early seventies, students were allowed to pray in school.

"Look," said Mom. She pointed around the room to the walls and windowsill loaded with cards. Most of them were from students at my school. "They're all for you, Beth." Their kindness touched me deeply.

I remember snatches of conversations with my parents before I drifted off to sleep again for hours at a time. The nurses took on the task of giving me sponge baths, so oftentimes I woke up quivering. At times the chills felt like bugs racing up my body.

> *Mom called the school and asked the teachers and students to pray for me.*

"Pops! Get the bugs off of me!" I yelled, even though he wasn't in my hospital room. Frantic, I pushed away the perpetrator, the washcloth. Bugs terrified me, like the ghosts at night; at home Pops always rescued me from being attacked by one of them. Bugs frightened me almost as much as the dark—almost.

The high fever lingered and my body ached. The nurse said that the IV attached to the bag of liquid put fluids in my body, yet I always woke up thirsty. Sometimes it hurt to be touched even by my bedsheets, yet I longed to be touched, especially by my parents. Night nurses did not visit my room as often as the day nurses, and I frequently woke up to an empty room at night. Even with the bathroom light and the side lights on to keep away the monsters, I felt scared and so alone.

At the time, I didn't realize that my parents were going through their own set of trials. Doctors told my parents that I wasn't sleeping, but rather was losing consciousness. The doctors had been searching for answers as to why I was so sick, but one week after my dad bolted into the emergency room with me in his arms, they still had no answers. After a week of tests, the doctors could not determine what was wrong, and they could not bring the fever down, even with the IV fluids and sponge baths. The doctors were baffled.

"Beth could die," the doctor finally told my parents.

The news shocked them, and my mother reached out for additional prayer from people in various churches and prayer chains. My mother notified every friend, neighbor, coworker, and family member to request prayer for me.

After the doctor's bad news, my mother began bringing me little figurines each day. She had collected about eight Easter rabbits. Each night before she left the hospital, she'd say, "Beth, I'll bring you another figurine tomorrow. You'll see then what it is. Just wait and see."

Mom told me later that she brought me a figurine each day to give me something to look forward to so that I'd fight to stay alive. Of course, I didn't know that the doctors told my parents that I could die, but I guessed that if my school was praying for me then I must be pretty sick. My pain level remained the same as it was before we left home. I wondered, *Aren't hospitals supposed to make you get better?*

One night when I was all alone, during a lucid moment, I decided to pray to God. Even though my family and I went to church most Sundays, all that I knew spiritually was that Jesus was born on Christmas (when I got all those presents) and He died on Easter. Of course, I also knew Noah had a boat with lots of animals and that Adam and Eve were two naked people who loved each other.

My dad was kind of a reluctant Christian, but my mom taught me that God watches over me and protects me. That's why we got down on our knees to say prayers before going to bed each night. I wasn't a very spiritual child, but tonight I felt desperate. Where was God now? I wondered why I wasn't getting any better, even though I had so many X-rays and blood tests. I felt a little worse, and that didn't seem right to me. Why wasn't God making me better?

I was just so tired and couldn't take it any longer. I said, "God, I'm ready to die now. Take away this pain."

After that, I lost consciousness again.

My Heavenly Experience

Suddenly, I felt a searing pain in my chest and it jolted me awake. But then the pain was gone and I felt wonderful! I hadn't felt this good since my birthday party, and I didn't want the feeling to end.

A golden light surrounded me. It was more of a glowing light, not like the light that the nurse left on in the bathroom. This light enveloped me—it seemed to be around me and inside of me all at once, and I couldn't even see that I was still in my hospital room. I wasn't afraid, though. I felt at peace.

The glow of the golden light dissipated a little bit so that I could see my hospital room again. I lay on my back, breathing easily without a mask, the pain all gone. I noticed a small light in the upper-right corner of the ceiling in my room. It was quite small, but it filled my soul with wonder; I couldn't take my eyes off of it. As I stared, the light got brighter and brighter and grew larger and larger.

As the light got closer, I could see a man walking toward me. It seemed like he was walking for a very long time, as though there were miles between us. When he finally arrived, he was floating in the air by my bed! He had brown hair and a beard and wore a brown robe. He had the most incredible eyes I had ever seen! They seemed to glow. He smiled at me and I smiled back. I felt loved and safe. I wasn't sure who he was, but it felt like I knew him somehow. This man was full of brightness and love. I wasn't afraid at all. I was fascinated!

He spoke without moving his mouth. I spoke back to him without moving my mouth too. We communicated with our thoughts; at the time, that seemed perfectly natural to me.

As the light got closer, I could see a man walking toward me. When he arrived, he was floating in the air.

"Are you ready to die?" he asked.

I felt like this man knew everything about me, even though I'd never met him before. Immediately, I answered, "No! I'm just a little girl. I haven't lived yet."

As soon as I said that I looked away for a minute. I thought, *That's strange. I just prayed and told God that I am ready to die.*

I looked back at the man and he smiled again—as if to reassure me that it was all right that I was honest and that I would be all right too. In fact, I felt very welcomed by him. In that moment, I believed there was nothing I could say that was wrong or childish or offensive. I'd never met anyone like him—an adult who seemed to know all about me and love me with such magnetic power.

We locked eyes. He asked, "What have you done with your life?"

I grinned. I was only nine years old! I wasn't sure what he wanted me to say. Then he showed me things—things that I could do for God and for people if I didn't die. The experience was intense and real.

He showed me things—things that I could do for God and for people if I didn't die.

The next thing I knew, the man was leaving, our conversation over. As he walked away, the light in the room diminished and returned to being a small dot in the corner of the room before it disappeared completely. A bit of pain returned, so I closed my eyes.

A Return to Reality

All of a sudden I was very much awake, standing in the middle of my bed! I woke up standing in my bed! The light in my hospital bathroom seemed very bright. I didn't feel so sick anymore! I jumped up and down on the bed, delighted to feel better. I had to tell someone what just happened to me!

I got on my knees and reached for the hospital phone and called the only number I knew by heart.

"Mom?"

"Beth! Beth, are you okay?" It was the middle of the night. Mom was surprised to hear my voice, but I was very excited.

"Mom, a man came to see me and asked me if I was ready to die."

My mother panicked to hear about an intruder. She hung up and immediately called the hospital. But I felt so good I jumped up and down on the bed again!

A flurry of nurses rushed into the room, flipped on every light, and looked frantically for the intruder.

"What did this man look like?" one asked. "Did you know him?" "What was his name?"

One nurse paid no attention to them. She had me sit down on the bed and slipped a thermometer in my mouth. Even with my mouth closed around the thermometer, the questions kept coming.

"Did he sit beside you?" "Did he try to hurt you?"

The nurse beside me pulled out the thermometer. "Her fever's broken."

Hands reached in to feel my forehead, fluff my pillow, and help me sit back. All the nurses huddled around my bed.

"A man came in here?" one of them asked.

I nodded.

"What did he look like?"

I told them about the bright light. Then I said, "He wore a brown robe and had brown hair and a beard. He had the most beautiful eyes."

"What did he say?"

"He asked if I was ready to die," I told them.

Their eyes got big.

"What else did he say?"

"He asked me, 'What have you done with your life?'"

When I said this, the nurses immediately froze all at the same moment. No one said, "Freeze!" like they do in the movies. Everyone just stopped moving. They looked the way you do in a game of freeze tag, only this time everybody was tagged all at once, stopped at the same moment. I thought they were acting weird.

Their eyes darted back and forth at one another. *Definitely weird.*

Many of them left, and I think one of them must have consulted with the doctor because soon I was being wheeled down the hall for yet another X-ray; they took more blood too.

My mother had to arrange for my little brothers to stay with someone the next day before she could come see me. As I waited for her, a bunch of other people began to arrive—a few priests, ministers, and a pair of nuns. They were armed with notepads and wanted to hear about the man in the brown robe. I repeated my story to each one.

> Priests, ministers, and a pair of nuns wanted to hear about the man in the brown robe.

My mother finally arrived. She kept touching my forehead, tears in her eyes because the fever was finally gone. The tests and extra visitors wore me out. I really didn't sleep the night before, plus the adrenaline that energized my euphoric bed jumping had vanished.

Every test taken after the visit from the man in the brown robe came back to reveal I had a severe case of pneumonia. Although the hospital had ordered the same X-rays, blood work, and tests previously, this time the pneumonia that nearly killed me showed up on every test.

After a blur of examinations, visitors, and extended rest, I woke up one day to see my dad sitting on my hospital bed, his head bent over a sketch pad, pencil in hand. It was a familiar sight and it comforted me. I wondered what he was drawing.

He grinned and handed me a picture. He signed it, "Beth in hospital—June 1970. Done by Jack." What a special memento of my life-changing experience.

Finally Home, but Changed Forever

Istayed in the hospital for a few more days and then was allowed to go home. I was pale, thin, and weak from the whole ordeal. The illness had taken a toll on me, and when I returned home, I was still an invalid. I had been in the hospital for so many weeks that school had let out for the summer before I got home.

Pops carried me up the stairs to my bedroom that first night. I pulled my pink quilt up to my chin and rubbed its soft fabric against my face. I breathed in the familiar smell of it, glad to be out of that hospital bed. After we said our prayers together, kneeling like we always do, Mom tucked me in and kissed my forehead.

"Good night, my Beth," she said. "It's so good to have you home again."

"Good night, Mom."

Mom turned and switched on the closet light.

"Mom?"

"Yes?"

"It's okay. You can leave the light off."

"Are you sure?" she replied. "You always want a light on, even at the hospital."

I nodded. "I'm not afraid of the dark anymore."

"Okay, Beth. If you're sure." She left the door open a crack and paused outside my door. I knew she was waiting for me to panic and cry like I used to when it was dark. But I really didn't even need a night-light. That intense fear of the dark, the monsters, and ghosts was gone—it went away when the man with the beard and fabulous eyes visited me in the hospital. I yawned and turned over on my side. I heard

Mom's slippers scuff the floor as she walked down the hall and I drifted off to sleep.

The next day, my first morning back home, I slept in late. Pops stayed home from work and carried me down the stairs. Mom made my favorite breakfast—bacon and homemade pancakes with butter and syrup. It tasted so good! Mom cleared the table as Pops made an announcement.

"Beth, your mother and I think that the fresh air will help you feel better. We set up a place for you to rest outside."

My heart leaped! I loved being outside!

"You want to see it?" he asked.

"You bet I do!"

I was happy to be outside, out of the hospital and in the shade of our backyard tree.

Pops carried me out the back door to the large tree that graced our backyard. He had tied a hammock up to the tree. I knew immediately that Mom had arranged the little table with books to read and color nearby.

I was so happy to be outside, away from the starchy white hospital sheets and in the shade of our backyard tree. The lovely fragrance of lily of the valley surrounded me as I lay in the hammock. I rested, smelled the flowers, read a little bit, and just watched the clouds float across the sky above my swing set.

My family fell into a routine. Every morning, I ate my breakfast and took my medicine, then if it wasn't raining, my father carried me outside and placed me in the hammock. Sometimes my brothers came outside to play and even tried to entertain me a time or two with their squirt guns. The cool water felt good, and I loved the sound of their laughter as they chased each other around me.

One day, my brother Scott brought me something he was sure would make me scream—a praying mantis. I was so afraid of bugs, but praying mantises were spooky looking, and I hated them the most.

"Look what I have for you, Beth," Scott teased. He cupped the long creature in both of his hands. "Want to hold him?"

"Sure," I replied. I held out my hands.

Scott's mouth dropped open. "What's changed you?"

I didn't answer him. I just let the praying mantis crawl all over my hands and forearm.

My mother asked me the same question later that day.

"Beth, Scott tells me that you held a praying mantis? What's going on? Since when aren't you afraid of bugs?"

"Insects are our friends, Mom," I replied.

Mom shook her head in disbelief.

In time, I was able to walk the long distance from our house to the hammock, even though it expended most of my energy. Mom was a teacher, so she stayed home with us during the summer. When Mom wasn't outside, she kept an eye on all of us from the window. Over the course of the day, she would walk out with a tray of drinks and snacks for all of us.

After my long hospital stay, I cherished my hours in the hammock. I even loved the bugs. I spied them on the tree bark, in the grass, and sometimes buzzing around my head. Somehow, I found a new appreciation for creation and studied each living thing that God made. More than anything, I loved the fragrances that wafted in the breeze as I lay there, rocking gently—or not so gently if my brothers ran by me. At first, it was just the fragrance from the lily of the valley, but as new summer flowers appeared, they delivered to me different fragrances, new color, and hope.

Now that no one was poking me or asking me questions every few minutes, I had time to think about the man who came to see me in the hospital. In some way, the earthy smell of my mother's vegetable garden, the fragrant flowers, and the skittering sound of squirrels racing over the leafy branches above me reminded me of his visit. There was something about him, a familiar feeling like I knew him from my past. *Who was he?* I thought. It occurred to me that the

> *There was something about him, a familiar feeling like I knew him from my past.*

nurses knew. They had to know something—they had acted so weird when I was telling them about the man in the brown robe. It was even more strange that priests and nuns came to visit me after I told the nurses about the man in the robe. I wondered if I would I see him again. If I did, would he ask me again what I'm doing with my life?

A Stunning Realization

One day while I was laying on the hammock in my backyard, surrounded with the fragrance of flowers, I realized that the man in the brown robe was Jesus. Immediately, something in me changed. I knew God wanted me to live.

Eventually, I resumed going to church with my family. Many people there told me they had been praying for me when I was in the hospital. If only they knew how incredibly God had answered their prayers! I was glad to go to church and found myself paying careful attention to the stories. More than ever before, I listened and asked questions in Sunday school. One question I wanted answered was why Jesus allowed Himself to be crucified. I came to realize that the world was transformed through Jesus when He did that for us.

I needed the entire summer to recuperate, but by the time school started, I was ready to return. At first the school days exhausted me. When my school pictures came back, I held mine up next to last year's picture. I looked so skinny and pale compared to last year, even after a full summer of rest. What was even more amazing, though, is that I wasn't shy in school anymore. I had a new confidence with my old friends and easily made new friends. Since I came home from the hospital I had changed, inside and out. I liked the new me!

I was in school for a few months before I finally felt ready to talk about my hospital experience—the time when I met the man with the brown robe, when I met Jesus. I went to talk to my mother.

"You know, Mom, I think I know who the man in the brown robe was," I said.

"Who?" my mom asked.

"It was Jesus," I said.

"I think so too," she replied, "but don't tell anybody." Mom never told me why she didn't want me to tell anyone.

At the time, I didn't intend to tell anyone but her. I also told her that the paintings that I saw in church of Jesus as being sickly are not really accurate. Jesus looked like a healthy man with kind eyes, and did not look like He had just been crucified. He was actually very healthy and well. I believed and trusted Him.

For years I followed my mother's advice and didn't tell anyone else about my experience. But Jesus's second question continued to direct my life in ways I'm still realizing.

Living a Life with Purpose

My life and everything that I do revolves around Jesus's question that day in the hospital: "What have you done with your life?" Before Jesus left my hospital room, I believe He revealed to me some choices I would make that would impact people.

As a child, I took piano lessons but eventually was able to teach myself. Family, neighbors, and friends loved to hear me play, and I loved playing for them. As a teenager I knew music was important to me. I studied music in college and was encouraged to train to become a concert pianist. Although I didn't pursue that as a profession, music continued to be a big part of my life.

I wasn't always paying attention to God, though. I have to admit that I tend to get caught up in my own life and my own needs, rarely looking out for anyone else. But the near-death experience from my childhood stuck with me and influenced me in times when I would have chosen to walk by someone in need, like the blind man I met one day.

After college, I got married and had two beautiful daughters. This was the early 1990s; we lived in Atlanta, Georgia, where I worked in public relations. I woke up late one morning—my alarm hadn't gone off for some reason. I ran out the door without breakfast and pulled into a parking space at work, stressed because I was late. My leg caught on the dashboard as I got out of my car and I ripped my pantyhose. As if that wasn't enough, I got to work and the coffeepot was broken. Now I'd missed breakfast and coffee.

I decided to walk to the mall in downtown Atlanta over my lunch hour to buy a coffee, lunch, and a new pair of hose. I'd have to hurry, but I could do it in an hour.

I practically ran out the door at noon. I waited at the street corner for the light to change. For some reason, the man beside me caught my attention. He had a white cane; a quick glance at his face revealed that his eyes had the white pupils that are characteristic of someone who is blind. *Could he possibly cross the street by himself?*

I looked around, hoping someone else would see that this man needed help. I did not feel like helping anyone. I was hungry and I desperately needed caffeine. Worse, it was embarrassing to walk in downtown Atlanta with a large hole in my pantyhose.

At that moment, the question the man in the brown robe asked me years ago as a child flooded over my soul: "What have you done with your life?" I paused. I thought about the kindness and love that I felt from him. I stepped toward the man and half-heartedly asked, "Do you need assistance?"

"Oh yes," he answered. "Would you help me cross the street?"

"Of course."

When the light changed, he held on to my arm. We slowly crossed the intersection, and all the while I was thinking how I was losing the time I needed to collect the things I wanted at the mall. I helped him get to the curb on the other side.

"Thank you, miss," he said.

"You're welcome," I answered. I started off toward the mall. I still had time to get there and back if I hurried—and if the other intersections weren't terribly jammed. I hesitated. *I can't just leave him there!* I felt terrible. I turned around.

"Where do you need to go?" I asked.

"To the mall."

Figures.

The man held my elbow with his fingers as I led him down the sidewalk, which was packed with pedestrians. I must admit I didn't feel like a Good Samaritan or a good Christian. I felt agitated as we walked the three blocks to the mall entrance. I kept wondering what sort of emergency would compel this man to walk through downtown Atlanta over lunch hour. Finally, my curiosity got the best of me.

"What are you planning on doing at the mall?"

"It is my friend's birthday and I want to get her a card," he said.

By now I thought I might as well ask what was really on my mind. "How can you come all the way to downtown Atlanta by yourself? How were you planning on crossing the street?"

The man said, "When I get to a street corner, I begin to pray and ask God to send a good person to help me. I then just stand there and wait until He sends the person He has chosen."

Oh my! I certainly did not see myself as the good person God sent to help a blind man. Had it not been for my encounter with Jesus as a child, I wouldn't have made any effort at all. I could almost taste the selfishness in my mouth. I learned his name was Frank. As we stepped into the mall, I stepped further outside my comfort zone.

"Would you like me to help you pick out a card for your friend?" I asked. This time I meant it. This time I wanted to be there. I realized God was watching and He really was interested in what I was doing with my life.

"Oh, could you? That would be wonderful," he exclaimed.

We walked into the Hallmark store and I read a few of the birthday cards and told him what picture was on the front. He chose a card with birds on it and plunked down twenty dollars at the register.

> *I realized God was watching and He was interested in what I was doing with my life.*

By this time, I had to get back to work. Lunch, coffee, and new pantyhose would have to wait. I knew I wanted to walk this man to the subway and send him on his way home. I marveled at the sunshine, the birds singing, and the wonder of having clear eyes to see it all. I thought about Jesus's words: "Again Jesus spoke to them, saying, 'I am the light of the world. Whoever follows me will never walk in darkness but will have the light of life'." (John 8:12, NRSV)

Frank walked in a physical darkness, but he had Jesus's light of life inside of him. Because I stopped to help him, I walked in the same light.

I helped Frank get on the subway and hurried back to the office. As soon as I walked in, my coworker said, "Hey, Beth, that's quite a hole you have there in your stocking."

I grinned. "Oh yes, thank you." *At least the hole in my heart is fixed,* I thought. I had no regrets. Had it not been for my near-death experience, I am pretty sure I would have left that blind man at the traffic light to fend for himself.

On another occasion, I was also in the middle of a busy intersection in Atlanta when I had the opportunity to think about someone other than myself.

I had been waiting with a handful of others for the crosswalk light to change so we could cross the intersection. We had just started when suddenly a car rounded the corner and hit a woman right in front of me. I gasped. She flew up over the top of the car and landed on the pavement.

> *Suddenly a car rounded the corner and hit a woman right in front of me.*

The woman lay on the pavement, stunned.

Before I could help the woman up, she stood to her feet.

"What are you doing?" I asked. "You need to sit down while we call an ambulance."

"No, I have to get to work," she said. She was dazed and obviously in shock.

"Okay, I'm going with you," I told her.

I told her coworkers that she had been hit by a car and left them my contact information. I found out later that the victim had broken ribs and a concussion, and suffered permanent hearing loss.

My mother used to say, "There but for the grace of God go I." She meant that being aware of others' suffering like the ones I witnessed could be my lot in life. I couldn't help but think that if I'd been walking a little faster or if the car were going a little slower, things would have been very different. It could have been me who sailed over the car and landed on the concrete. I learned from the man in the brown robe with kind eyes that my purpose on this earth is to love people.

More Life Changes

Years after I returned from my NDE I started to remember new things from that experience as my life unfolded. I recall being told about my children and also that I would one day become ill with a debilitating disease. People describe having feelings of déjà vu. When I was diagnosed in the mid-1990s with multiple sclerosis (MS), I wasn't surprised since it was revealed to me in my NDE that my life would not be perfect or without pain.

MS, a potentially disabling disease of the brain and spinal cord, disrupts communication between the brain and the rest of the body. For me, the initial onset of MS presented itself as small, or petit absence, seizures. The first time it happened, I blacked out while driving in Atlanta and almost wrecked my car. At first I was diagnosed as an epileptic. I learned to detect when a seizure was coming on through an aura and an identifiable sound. I'd stop driving until the episode was over. By the time I got a second opinion and the MS was diagnosed, the seizures had stopped.

While the diagnosis was life changing for me, not all of the changes were bad. When I first entered adulthood, the intensity of my NDE had lessened somewhat. I had strayed a bit from my relationship with God, and I am actually thankful that He rescued me from thinking too highly of myself.

Shortly after my diagnosis, in April 1998, we moved to Grand Rapids, Michigan. It actually snowed! I thought to myself in a panic, *What have I done?*

But God had a plan for us in Grand Rapids, and today I like it better than any other place I've lived. Maybe that's because one of my most memorable events happened on a snowy day in Grand Rapids.

I had stopped at a gas station and carefully stepped out of my car. Snow and ice were everywhere, so I used my cane to steady myself, pumped the gas, and carefully walked around the slippery parts as I hobbled inside the store to pay cash.

An elderly woman stood at the counter in front of me.

"Can you put air in my tires?" she asked the attendant. "I'm afraid I don't know how to do it."

"I'm sorry," the attendant answered. "I'm not allowed to leave my cash register."

I looked around. The store was full of customers but only one person behind the counter. *I should help her. But how?* I argued with myself. When you have any kind of disability, it can be tempting to focus on what you can't do. I kept arguing with myself: *You're handicapped! You could get hurt going out there in this snow. Let someone else do it. You can't.*

Suddenly, I heard a thought so loud that I looked around to see who was talking. I heard, "Get your buns out there." It sounded like something my mother would say and I made my decision. I was going to help this elderly woman put air in her tires.

We kind of leaned on each other as we inched our way across the lot to the air pump. I hung on to the side of her car and removed the little cap.

"See, you take it off like this and make sure you put it in a safe place, up here on the hood maybe."

I demonstrated the entire procedure, then asked her, "Who usually does this for you?"

"Oh, my husband usually does that for me."

I said, "Where is he now?"

She burst into tears. "In the funeral home. That's where I'm going now, to make arrangements."

Now I *knew* that God wanted me to help this woman. "Can I give you a hug?"

"Yes."

We hugged out there in that frigid gas station parking lot for about a minute. I had a doctor's appointment to go to or I would have gone to the funeral home with her because she was all alone.

I was no hero. At first I wasn't even willing to help. It was icy and freezing cold, and I didn't want to help that woman. I was being selfish. That voice in my head telling me to get my buns out there was clearly direction from God.

> *I knew that God wanted me to help this woman. He knew she needed someone.*

Jesus knew she needed someone, but He knew I had a need too—to love and help people in need.

Shortly after we moved to Grand Rapids, I worked a side job as a stringer reporter for the local newspaper. But my greatest joy was teaching music to kindergarten through seventh grade students in a school for disabled children. Ken-o-sha Elementary School in Grand Rapids, Michigan, was well known. I was honored to teach children with various types of disabilities such as cerebral palsy, autism, blindness, Down syndrome, and physical impairments that required them to use a walker or a wheelchair. God gave me the opportunity to work with these children not only to share with them the gift of music but also to feel love and support from those around them. This was especially true for a young blind girl who touched me deeply.

Sadly, I couldn't continue teaching at the school. I got too sick. After a time, I couldn't even play the piano anymore because my hands wouldn't cooperate.

A New Life

Before my MS diagnosis, I was a bit full of myself. I was adventurous, performed in musical theater, and excelled in my career. After I was diagnosed, I eventually lost everything—my looks, my ability to stay fit, my ability to play the piano, my ability to use my college degrees, and my ability to drive a car using my feet. I even lost my marriage.

> My experience with the man in the brown robe changed how I look at this new life.

But my experience with the man in the brown robe changed how I look at this new life. To this day, I still am not afraid of insects or the dark. I have become even more confident and more caring. I even wrote a best-selling book about MS. I am very different from the timid little girl that I used to be.

Even though my MS will worsen, I believe God must have something else He wants me to do. Every day, I am excited to see what He has in mind for me to accomplish.

At the end of the day, Jesus's question rings in my ears. "What have you done with your life?" It was a question for me and yet is a question for every one of us. It is a question to be lived day by day, week by week, year by year until at last I see Him again, face to face. What a day that will be!

My Life since My Near-Death Experience

Beth Praed

Just when I think God has shown me everything He has in store for me or wants me to do, something else happens and I realize His work—my work—isn't done.

Q How did your NDE change your relationship with God?

A I truly believe that the day of my NDE I was born again. I started believing in God—not because my mom had taught me to, but because I wanted God to be an essential part of my life.

That day Jesus saved me in two ways. First, I truly believe that He saved me from my sins when He died on the cross. Second, He saved me from dying when He came to me in my hospital room.

I realized then, too, that there was a reason God allowed me to come back. I wasn't just saved from dying, but I also was saved to fully live out the rest of my life with purpose. I knew that my life on earth would have meaning and God would use me to help people. I think that's why I had shouted, "I want to live!"

Q Many experiencers reveal that they returned with a greater sense of love and peace. Did you? If so, how have those feelings influenced your life?

A When I awoke in my hospital bed after my NDE, I felt more love and joy than I ever thought possible. I was also pain-free and fearless of things that scared me before my experience. Once I had time to process what happened and realized that I saw and talked to Jesus, I also felt more confident as a child. These feelings deepened as I got older, had my children, and embraced both joys and struggles in my life.

Q *During your NDE, did you see glimpses of the future? If so, have those glimpses come true?*

A I didn't realize that I had glimpsed the future during my NDE until things happened to me afterward, such as my MS diagnosis. When the seizures started and tests were being run, I remembered that Jesus told me that I would be ill with a debilitating disease, that I would live with pain. Yet my MS has reminded me that God has a plan. I know that God's plan for me is to be a caring, loving person toward others, especially those in need.

Ever since that day on the hammock in my backyard, just after I got home from the hospital, I have asked myself the same question: What does God want me to do today? I try to live my life guided by that question.

Q *Why do you think you had a near-death experience?*

A People ask me why I think God let me have a near-death experience. I honestly don't know. I don't think I am special, but I do believe that individuals who have a near-death experience possess a unique way of seeing the world. We don't judge others. We are often kind and understanding of an individual's difficulties because we've been baptized in a love that is otherworldly, a love that belongs to God.

And let's not forget faith. We have a tremendous amount of faith that God is with us all the time and that the ways in which we live our lives will count here and in the next world too. While I am alive, I want to do my best to make my life worth God's gift to me.

A Message of Love

By Nadia McCaffrey, as told to Anita K. Palmer

Love and compassion are necessities, not luxuries.
Without them humanity cannot survive.

Dalai Lama

The light was brighter than the sun. But I was not blinded by it. I was being drawn into it. I was floating in it. The whole me—whatever "me" means—longed to be immersed in it, to be a part of it forever. It was love. It was everything.

It grew bigger and bigger. I was only seven years old, but I was not afraid. Then the light shimmered and transformed into the shape of a being. A dazzling, magnificent, regal female figure all in white. Her form appeared to be covered in a gossamer robe tied with a glowing cord around the middle. A sparkling blue material draped her head and shoulders.

Her presence conveyed compassion and understanding and acceptance. Unconditional love—what every human being hungers for. I felt it from every particle of everything I could see. The colors emanating from this figure were hues I had never seen before and have never seen since. I sensed that they had meanings, but I couldn't tell what they were. I don't have memories based on other senses, like smell or hearing—but the moment was huge and deep and beautiful.

The woman's arms reached outward but they did not touch me. Instead, a feeling of serenity and limitless security enveloped me. I felt like a newborn baby in front of an immense being of love.

Without using a voice, she spoke. *"Je suis ta Petite Maman du Ciel,"* she said. I am your Little Mother of the Sky.

> *She let me know I was going to have to return to my body and continue life on earth.*

As I started to ponder that, she continued to communicate. She let me know I was going to have to return to my body and continue life on earth. There were things I had to learn, things I had to do.

She added phrases and concepts I could not comprehend—metaphorical and symbolic and prophetic ideas my childlike mind could not grasp.

Then she communicated these words: "In the middle of a garden, you will see a rose, more colorful and beautiful than all others. When the time comes, you will open yourself to others and share this message of love. *Me parler est prier. Prier est aimer.* To speak to me is prayer, and to pray is to love."

She also said I would be fine. My leg would heal, and I would continue in life to accomplish my mission.

"I will be with you always," was the last thing she said. Then the light faded and she was gone.

Chosen by God

I am in my midseventies now. I have lived decades since I was that little girl surrounded by heavenly light. I married and raised a child.

I traveled the world. I have tried to love as *Maman du Ciel* commanded. I do not know why God chose me to have three near-death experiences (NDEs) and many other spiritual encounters that I cannot fully describe. I also don't know why I am still on earth.

I was born in France in 1945, just after the end of World War II. My mother's family lived in beautiful Auvergne, in the central region of the country. Now called Auvergne-Rhône-Alpes, it's a mostly rural area that is still largely undiscovered by tourists even though it boasts rugged hills, forests, and rivers. The Auvergne was the home of Blaise Pascal, the seventeenth-century Christian apologist, mathematician, and inventor who wrote his famous *Pensées*. (It is also known as a setting in Anne Rice's vampire stories!)

An abundance of natural hot springs has spawned spa towns, such as the beautiful, ancient Vichy, known for its art and mineral water and called the queen of France's historic walled cities. Founded by the Romans on the banks of the Allier River, Vichy was associated over the centuries with notable French aristocrats like the Marquise de Sévigné in the 1600s; Lafayette, who fought on the American side of the Revolutionary War; and the last monarch of France, Napoleon III, who established Vichy as a cultural center.

This town formed the backdrop of my childhood. My maternal grandparents, my *memée* and *pépe*, who mainly raised me, lived outside Vichy. Their large house, surrounded by gardens full of old trees and lilac bushes, was on a hill above the nearby village. Over the centuries it had been converted from a chapel into a convent and then an estate. Rolling wheat fields surrounded it, lined by ancient rock walls. It was my favorite place in the world. I would wander alone for hours.

Memée and Pépe owned five farms. They managed to operate them throughout the war despite some of the land lying in German-occupied territory. Pépe, a wounded veteran of World War I, would travel on both sides of the Demarcation Line, building relationships with the German soldiers at checkpoints so that they would not suspect him of working with the resistance and smuggling Jews into free France.

I adored Memée and Pépe and spending time at their home. I loved my mother and father, but I did not see them much. They were busy all the time. When I was four years old, they sent me to a nearby Roman Catholic boarding school. We know now that age is way too young to be away from parents, but people thought differently back then. The school was very strict and I struggled. One year, I think it was Easter vacation, my parents actually forgot to pick me up. Thank goodness Pépe came and got me.

A Life-Changing Moment

I loved staying with Memée and Pépe at their estate during school vacations and holidays. Then came a day that I shall always remember: July 7, 1952.

My grandmother loved flowers. Despite the blazing midday heat, I decided I would go make her a bouquet of bachelor's buttons, sweet pea, and poppies. As I zigzagged down the hillside, I was humming and full of happiness.

Past a small grove of wild cherry trees, I reached the timeworn stone retaining wall that was built with material from an old medieval tower. I climbed to the top. On the other side was a field, a sea of waving grain. I scanned for flowers. There! I spotted some. They looked glorious but a long way away. For just a moment I hesitated. I would need to bush-whack through the golden stalks, which were as tall as I was, but I told myself to just do it.

I hopped off the wall and began to weave through the wheat. Then I looked down. Partially hidden at my feet was a dark shape. A venom-ous asp! I froze. For a long moment, the deadly snake looked at me. Then it buried its fangs above my left ankle. I remember screaming. Later I learned that people working in nearby fields a mile away heard the scream.

The creature slithered away. The pain was so intense my vision started to dim. I screamed again, as loudly as I could with my little-girl voice. "Memée! Memée!" I was horrified to see blood dripping from the bite. My heart was racing. I managed to crawl back over the rock wall and began to stagger up the hill toward home.

I screamed one more time. The pain was atrocious. My leg was so heavy! I collapsed in the warm grass. My grand-mother had heard me and came rushing down from the farmhouse.

The deadly snake looked at me, then it buried its fangs above my left ankle.

"*Unserpent m'a mordu!*" I whispered. A snake bit me.

"Oh, *mon Dieu!*" Memée cried. She whipped off her black apron and ripped off the ties to use as a tourniquet, twisting them with a stick. Then she put her lips to the two-inch-wide wound on the side of my calf and sucked, hoping to remove the venom. Of course, it was too late—running had shot the poison throughout my body.

Memée carried me up to the house and yelled for Pépe. They had no telephone in their old home. Pépe hurried away on his bicycle to the nearest phone he could find, more than two kilometers from the house. It would take an hour before he would be able to call a doctor to come.

As my grandmother laid me on the chaise lounge in the main room, I was violently ill, vomiting, passing in and out of consciousness. Two hours later, the first doctor arrived. His wife stayed in their car, crying and refusing to come in because she knew I had to be dead. Then a second doctor arrived with my mother, who worked for him. I didn't remember any of this.

> *The doctor didn't know I was going to become a miracle child.*

The first doctor decided to inject my abdomen with an antivenom shot even though the other doctor protested that it was too late. He was right, in human terms. But he didn't know I was going to become a miracle child.

After the Light

Everyone had expected me to die. I was unconscious when they moved me into my grandparents' bedroom. Eventually, after lying in a coma for ten days, I awoke. Everyone was stunned! There were many tears shed and prayers of gratitude uttered and rosaries said. It was unexplainable.

I learned that my grandparents bore most of the burden of taking care of me. Memée had a reputation in the region as a healer, using herbs, touch, and prayer to help people heal, and I'm certain that made a difference. My mother helped when she could, and some village friends came as well, but my grandparents kept most of the townspeople away.

My leg remained swollen for at least a month. My grandmother told me that the doctors had said I might need to have my leg amputated.

"No, you're not going to cut off my leg!" I said.

"Well, we hope not," she said. "But it's a possibility."

"No!" I said. "I'm going to learn to walk again! You'll see!"

I did, but not without months of Memée's nursing and me gaining strength and exercising. After two months, I could walk with a cane. It took a long time to return to running and playing as before, but I did. My leg bore a small scar but healed completely.

I knew it would heal because I had been sent back to earth to accomplish things. I needed to discover what they were, but I knew I was supposed to grow up.

A Difficult Childhood

No one who has had a near-death experience wants to return to this life. The "other place" is where we are meant to be. It is very hard to come back because we come out of the experience being changed on so many levels. It's a trauma, really. But being back in "reality" is traumatic too.

It's hard enough for an adult. Imagine it for a seven-year-old child who does not have the knowledge and wisdom with which to process the experience. When something so all-encompassing happens, it changes a person forever. The childhood years after my near-death experience were very difficult.

For one thing, when the beautiful heavenly being of light—based on my Roman Catholic upbringing, I came to believe she was the Blessed Virgin Mary—said she was always going to be with me, I as a little girl took that literally. Of course, she meant *spiritually*, but I recall feeling so disappointed for years as I slowly realized my Mother of the Sky would not be a constant physical companion. All I knew was that I wanted to be in the arms of Maman du Ciel.

I returned to the boarding school, where I was a nightmare for the nuns. I already was the type of person to question authority, but after the NDE, *mon Dieu*. I loved the sisters; they were wonderful. But I didn't listen. I didn't obey. I no longer saw things the same way as everyone else.

> *Death is not final.*
> *It is not something*
> *to be afraid of.*

The sisters would teach something as fact, and I would know it to be untrue. Not everything, just some things. For example: death. It is not final. It is not something to be afraid of. The space between *here* and *there*, between life and what we call death, is so thin. I never have found the right words to explain this. You almost can see through it, like a veil. Death is not the end of anything. It's just another level. It's just another place.

Occasionally, I would discern a hint of a presence during these years after my childhood NDE. An example is what happened when I was confirmed at age eleven. In the Roman Catholic Church, confirmation is a sacrament of initiation that completes baptism through the sealing of the Holy Spirit in the newly confirmed person's heart. Each child kneels in front of the bishop on the steps to the altar. I remember bending down. All of a sudden, a bolt of light struck me. I must have passed out because the next thing I remember is my grandfather at my side.

"Where is it?" I asked him.

"What?" he said.

"The Holy Ghost," I replied.

That's all I remember. No one had an explanation for the light or for my fainting. I stored the experience in my memory along with my visit with Maman du Ciel.

At school, the Mother Superior took me under her wing. She was called *Mére Marie de Angeles:* Mother Mary of the Angels. Once, at some point in the middle grades when I had been called to the office about some sort of bad behavior, she looked at me kindly and asked, "Do you want to share what happened?"

I somehow knew she was not asking about what had happened that day; she meant something bigger. I decided to tell her a little bit about the NDE. I was so happy when she did not reject it or criticize me. She simply accepted my account. From that point on she was there for me.

Later, when I was seventeen I decided to share my NDE with my grandmother. Memée said she had had a feeling that something had occurred after I had been bitten. But she told me to keep silent.

"Don't ever tell anyone about this," she said. "They won't understand. They'll think you are crazy."

Earlier, the Mother Superior had also told me to remain silent. I obeyed them, except with one person—my mother. Looking back, I don't know what motivated me. We weren't close. But when I was seventeen I shared a few details. She seemed to understand. I'm pretty sure she must have had a near-death experience herself and told no one. But I regret to say that I never asked.

It would be three decades—after I had grown up and married, moved with my American husband to Santa Cruz, California, and had my son—before I told anyone else.

A Growing Hunger for Heaven

My hunger for heaven became overwhelming in large part because I missed Maman du Ciel. But my disdain for life here deepened as well. My anger and rebellion, and *the waiting*, colored everything. I waited for Maman du Ciel to come see me or to call me to heaven. I felt lost because she did not. The images in my memory and the urges in my heart were like a huge magnet. I couldn't shake them loose; nothing on earth measured up, and I struggled to submit to a conventional, less-than existence.

> *Nothing on earth measured up, and I struggled to submit to a conventional, less-than existence.*

I had an overwhelming perception that the world was full of dishonesty and greed. It was as if my intuitive senses had multiplied.

On top of this, and perhaps because of it, I pushed people away. I was popular and my friends liked being around me. But I did not let anyone get close. My best friend stopped talking to me because I did not want to open up to her. I stayed connected to my grandparents, but I felt distant from my mother and father, to whom I could no longer relate. I never really had much of a relationship with my mother, but by this point I had basically stopped talking to her altogether. I was lonely.

I grew more reckless. I knew what awaited me in the hereafter and I didn't want to stay here. I decided to take matters into my own hands. If Maman du Ciel wouldn't come to me, I would go to her.

"You Cannot Stay"

I planned it all out. I chose a day when school was on a vacation break and I could be at my grandparents' home alone. I gathered all the pills I could find in the house—perhaps fifteen bottles in all. I didn't even know what they were. I put my hair up in an elegant style I had learned from my cousin. I selected a beautiful ballroom gown mostly black with lots of lace, and put on a lot of jewelry. I was determined to look like a princess. After all, I was going to see the queen of heaven.

While I regretted having to leave my family behind, I was so excited to finally return to my true home. I swallowed all the pills quickly. The world faded away.

God had other plans, though. A girl I knew from the village decided to return a book she had borrowed. Her boyfriend waited in the car while she let herself in and called my name. She found me, unconscious, sprawled across my bed.

My grandparents' farmhouse still didn't have a telephone. There was no such thing as a mobile phone, of course. And even if a call could have been made, there were no American-style 911 emergency services. My friend could only run down to get her boyfriend. Together they tugged me off the bed onto the floor. Then they dragged me by my feet down the stairs, one step at a time—I would have bruises all over to prove it!—and out the door to the car. They wrestled me into the back seat and raced down the estate entrance to the main road to Vichy, to the hospital fifteen kilometers (almost ten miles) away.

By the time I was examined, my heart had stopped. The doctors and nurses pumped my stomach and tried to restart my heart. But it did not beat again. A doctor declared me dead.

Only my body was dead, though. As before, I hovered above my form. I could see it on a hospital gurney, with doctors and nurses rushing around, trying to revive me. I found the scene uninteresting. I eagerly looked around for the light. But this experience was completely different from my first one.

> *I was sucked through something like a tunnel and almost spit out into a light.*

I was sucked through something like a tunnel and almost spit out into a light. It was a different color than the one in my first NDE. I found myself alone. I didn't see any beings or even hints of beings. I felt out of place, as if I wasn't supposed to be there. That's because I wasn't.

A deep, all-encompassing masculine voice filled my awareness and commanded my attention. It boomed around me like light bouncing off the surface of a diamond.

"You cannot stay. You have not even begun your work. You must go back."

The tone carried no judgment or condemnation.

The voice was so authoritative that I knew there would be no discussion. I could argue with anyone—priests, nuns, my grandparents, the police—but I could not argue with this voice. I had to go back.

I can't describe the depth of disappointment I felt as I once again hovered over my body, draped with a sheet. A nurse, an older woman, was sitting next to the gurney, crying. I assume she was keeping watch until orderlies came to take the body to the morgue and my grandparents could be notified. I was sucked back into my body. It was extremely fast, extremely brutal, really. It hurt.

I moved, and the nurse jumped up and screamed, and then began to cry with joy.

I, on the other hand, lay there with an overwhelming sense of failure, rejection, disappointment, sadness, and dread. No Maman du Ciel. I couldn't believe I had been sent back. I didn't understand. I felt like I did all that for nothing.

A Special Awareness

After my second NDE, my ability to sense things and my extraordinary awareness grew. I would just know things, suddenly, often about strangers. I could detect their energy, whether it was positive or negative. And with some people, I could discern something about them, such as if they were going to fall in love or how they were going to die. Not when but how.

Being young, I found it exciting to be able to do this. I wasn't aware that whatever information was being given me might not be welcomed by the person involved. I thought surely people would want to know. But that was not always the case.

One day, when I was about eighteen, I was walking down a street in Vichy. It was soon after my adventure with the pills. A young woman was coming toward me, and an awareness came to me. The thought brought joy, which I decided I should share. So I didn't hesitate to stop her.

"*Bonjour,*" I said. "I'd like to let you know that you have a new addition coming to your family. You're going to have a baby soon."

I never will forget the woman's face. She stared at me like I was absolutely crazy and started to walk backward from me, horrified. Then she turned and practically ran away.

I stood there stunned. How could that be her reaction to happy news? I didn't understand. Apparently knowing the future wasn't always welcome.

That's when I started to think that I had better keep my mouth shut. I could see that it could hurt—that I could hurt a lot of people unknowingly. Including my mother.

I learned how my mother was going to die. Without realizing the impact, I told her. It scared her. She never told me or showed me but I knew afterward. Even now I look back and think, *mon Dieu*, how could I have been so cruel? Can you imagine? I should never have said anything.

I had seen the disease, the blood, the suffering. It happened as I saw. At thirty-nine she was diagnosed with leukemia and in three months she was gone.

Paris, Marriage, and America

For many young people, the transition from adolescence to adulthood is not easy. At this stage of life I seemed to make it even more difficult.

My life had been very strict from every direction. Much more than my little brother, Christian, who was twelve and didn't have to go to boarding school. My parents, although in and out of my life, were strict with me; my grandparents were also strict; and of course, the Catholic boarding school was *very* strict! I was hungering for freedom.

So I got this idea. Back then in France, people were not independent until age twenty-one. But if they were under that age and divorced, then they were emancipated. All I had to do was find a man who would marry me and then divorce him. And that's what I did.

Looking back, I am appalled at my behavior. It's embarrassing to admit. But at the time, I didn't give any thought to whether it was bad or good. I was headstrong and determined.

Just after I graduated from high school, I won first prize in a Vichy beauty competition. I caught the eye of a nice gentleman, a businessman who was twenty years older than me. His maturity impressed me—I had no interest in teenage boys my age. I liked him at first and agreed to marry him. It wasn't long before I felt trapped again, and within the year I left him.

> *My parents, my grandparents, and the Catholic boarding school were very strict. I was hungering for freedom.*

I moved to Paris, where I had some relatives and a few acquaintances. I got a partial scholarship to study fashion; my parents paid for everything else except room and board. I got a part-time job in a café, and that is where I met the man who would become my second husband, Bob McCaffrey.

Bob worked at the US embassy in Paris. We dated for two years. I began to think about the future and get serious about life. I couldn't let myself do whatever crazy thing popped into my head. I left the fashion institute. I introduced Bob to my family, and we got married in Vichy.

Several months later Bob was discharged and wanted to take his bride home, to the United States. If I had known what it would mean for this French girl to marry this tall, handsome army sergeant and move to America, I don't think I could have done it. Bob was a good man, and together we had a wonderful son, Patrick. But by leaving France, I lost everything I had known. I can blame no one but myself. I was not there when my parents died. My brother felt abandoned and never forgave me. In fact, he stopped communicating with me. I never saw Memée and Pépe again. My culture, my way of life, was gone.

> *I vaguely knew I was somehow supposed to serve people in love, but I had no one to talk to about it.*

We settled in Northern California in 1968. I was twenty-three. Culturally, the whole Western world was in tumult. I was too. The sixties radically changed society, its morality, expectations, relationships, customs, everything. Whether or not that made it a little easier for me to adjust to the United States and marriage, I don't know. I do know that whatever spiritual gifts I had, I completely ignored them. I never mentioned NDEs to anyone, including Bob. I vaguely knew I was somehow supposed to serve people, but I had no one to talk to about it. I tried very much to forget about everything that had happened to me as a child.

Finding a Mission

Not surprisingly, I felt lonely and isolated. But I threw myself into being a mother. Patrick was born in 1970 at the hospital at Stanford University. He grew up in Sunnyvale.

We moved into a neighborhood where everybody knew one other. All the families had children about the same age, and they practically grew up together.

There were older folks around too. Many households had extended family members. It was the way people used to live. I miss that.

Across the street from us lived a Russian family. The grandmother lived with them, and she was dying. She was ready to go. I visited and noticed that the family members didn't really know how to handle the situation. The grandmother wanted things a certain way and I guess the family was too busy or too impatient to make it happen.

I listened to the grandmother and tried to gently advocate for her. I guess they appreciated it, because they asked if I would be willing to come and help. So I did. I just sat with her and let her talk. All she really wanted was to be close to her family, especially her grand-children, as the process of dying played out. I asked her for all her wishes, and then I passed the details to her sons and daughter-in-law. They discussed things and made changes. They put a hospital bed in one of the main living areas so that she could watch the children play-ing around her and her daughter-in-law cooking. She could interact and enjoy being part of the family. That's how she died, and I helped until the end.

Then another neighbor heard about it. The family lived on the same side of the street. The old lady there was just at the edge of turning a hundred years old. She spoke only Castilian Spanish but as a French speaker I could understand everything she said. She had had a fantastic life. Again, I just sat there and let her talk and was with her until she passed away as well.

I guess I got a reputation. It happened again and again—people asked for my help when their loved ones were dying. Being with people at the end of their life made me feel good. I always seemed to know what to do, how to help, how to communicate with them, how to ease their passing. So I thought, *Well, if it's the case, then I just better volunteer for a hospice organization or go to a nursing home and do some work there.* So I did.

Perhaps this was my mission, I thought. I remembered Maman du Ciel telling me I was supposed to do something to help people. Slowly I began to let myself recall the experiences of my childhood. I could see the connection between them and this new area of service. Still, I told no one.

A Change of Life

Unfortunately, my marriage to Bob was unraveling. Maybe I was too passionate about my work. I don't know exactly what it was, but in 1981, we decided to separate. Patrick was twelve.

I took the opportunity to do something very different. I found a job far away. In Tahiti! In many ways it was a logical choice. French is the primary language there, and my brother had served there with the French navy.

For three years I managed guest relations at a five-star resort on a lagoon. I loved it. Patrick lived with me for the first two years, spending vacations with his father in California. Then he wanted to switch the arrangement, to live with his dad and visit me in Tahiti on school breaks.

I missed Patrick so much. He and I were very close. We didn't have to talk in great detail to understand each other. We were open and honest with each other.

Even so, I had not told him much about my childhood near-death experiences. Just a mention in passing when he was in elementary school, but he began asking questions about God. He had been baptized in the Roman Catholic Church and taught the basics of Christianity, but I didn't force him in any direction. He had a deep belief in God and was very loving toward others.

As it turned out, he was more aware of spiritual things than I even imagined. After I returned from Tahiti, Patrick and I were talking one morning at breakfast before he left for high school. He got an odd look on his face and said, "Mom, you're going to be really mad at me tonight."

Patrick had a deep belief in God. He was more aware of spiritual things than I imagined.

I had no idea what he was talking about. "Why?" I asked. "What did you do?"

"I didn't do anything, but you will be mad at me tonight because of something that's going to happen," he said. I couldn't get more out of him, and he left for school in his red Mustang.

Around three-thirty that afternoon he called. "Mom, can you come and pick me up, please?"

I suddenly felt very apprehensive. "Why?" I asked.

"I had a car accident," he replied.

I drove like a crazy woman to his location. Thank God he was okay, but my first reaction was to be upset with him. He looked at me and said, "Mom, I told you you'd get mad."

I stopped and stared at him. He had known. How had he known? "Oh, *mon Dieu*," I said. "Tell me. I will listen."

He explained that somebody had run a stop sign and T-boned his Mustang in the middle of the intersection. Thankfully, the other driver also was unhurt. Patrick's car was totaled.

After this we talked. "How did you know?" I asked.

He said, "Well, I know things." He told me about some of his dreams and a sense of foreknowledge. He also shared about the time a few years earlier when he had been in a coma. He had had what he felt like was a visit to heaven.

Patrick's Experience

I was astounded. I remember that coma. He had been fifteen. After returning to California to live with his dad, Patrick had developed anorexia nervosa. (That's the main reason I came back from Tahiti.) I think it was the stress of the divorce. I felt terrible about it. It was severe to a point where he wasn't eating; he wasn't even drinking water. One day he fell and went into a coma and was hospitalized for a while.

During his coma, Patrick was told he was going to die young.

It was a long, long road back. I told him, "I'm going to be with you all the way with this." I didn't judge him; I just encouraged him.

He promised me that he was going to get healthy. He and I always gave our word to each other. When we said we would do something, we always did it.

His recovery was day by day. He wanted to cook his own food, and he started with rice and steamed fish. That went on for a while, and I was happy he was eating. Then he started going to a gym. As he improved physically, he also began to heal emotionally. He was on his way.

During his coma, he told me, he learned something else, something that didn't scare him but left him curious. He was told he was going to die young.

Unfortunately, the foreknowledge would prove to be correct.

A Calling to Minister

It was 1986, and I realized that all my experiences were leading me to care for terminally ill people and their families. I decided to start a business that was more than a hospice service. It would be that plus a source of training and education. I launched a 501(c)(3) nonprofit in Northern California called Angelstaff.

For eighteen years, my staff and I would go wherever we were asked to go—house, apartment, nursing home, or hospital—as long as we had the family's permission and participation. We trained over a thousand people on the process of death and dying. I lectured and gave presentations. I built connections with an international network of people involved in hospice care. More than anything else, I wanted to help prioritize the dying person first and the family second.

My company's philosophy was modeled after many leaders in the field, but I was greatly influenced by Dr. Elisabeth Kübler-Ross. I studied the psychiatrist and hospice pioneer's teachings and incorporated them into our program. I actually had quite an extensive exchange with Dr. Kübler-Ross by email before she died, and I talked with her by telephone. Interestingly, she shared that she, too, had had a near-death experience and became an expert on NDEs as well.

Over those nearly two decades, I helped countless families prepare for their loved one's passing. I sat with many people as they left this world. I have so many wonderful, magnificent experiences of witnessing people crossing to the other side, a place I know exists firsthand.

Discovering People Like Me

Despite spending so many years being involved with the dying, I still hadn't told anyone about my NDEs. I'd heard no one else describe anything like them, and I didn't think anyone would understand and would pass judgment. I kept my experiences buried deep. That was until I happened to notice a book in a bookshop in Santa Cruz in 1995.

> *I told no one about my NDEs. I didn't think anyone would understand and would pass judgment.*

Saved by the Light: The True Story of a Man Who Died Twice and the Profound Revelations He Received, by Dannion Brinkley (written with Paul Perry), had recently been published and had become a media sensation. As soon as I scanned the book, I felt a thrill of energy from my head to my toes. I found a chair in the corner of the bookstore and speed-read the entire book. I was overwhelmed with relief and joy and excitement.

I realized someone had experienced something very similar to what I did. *Oh my goodness,* I thought, *I am not alone!*

I need to talk to this man, I told myself.

As "luck" would have it, Brinkley was touring the country promoting the book, and he was scheduled to speak that month just thirty miles away in San Jose. I quickly bought a ticket. Because of *Saved by the Light's* international popularity, the event was attended by at least a thousand people. I don't like to be around crowds, but I was determined to sit in the front row and connect with this man.

Somehow I did just that. I found a seat close to the podium. As Brinkley took the microphone, I closed my eyes and meditated on the thought of talking to him. I didn't listen to him; I just kept meditating and envisioning talking with him. When I opened my eyes, he had stopped talking and was staring at me. He continued to speak but stopped again and stared. This happened three or four times.

I thought if I waited in line with his fans he might remember me and I would be able to ask a few questions. But as I said, I don't like crowds, so I found a back exit and went looking for where they were selling his book. He must have seen me walk out. The next thing I knew he was running after me! He took my hand, grabbed me around my waist, and kind of pulled me along to the book table. He wouldn't let go of my hand! I began to try to ask my questions. Then he stopped and looked at me again, deeply. Tears came into his eyes and he hugged me.

It was all a bit much for me. As soon as I could break away, I left. But the encounter was a turning point. From that point on I jumped with both feet into the world of experiencers and NDE researchers and began to realize there were many people like me. I attended meetings and read books and listened to lectures. I became involved with the International Association for Near-Death Studies (IANDS), which is very well respected. Names became acquaintances; acquaintances became co-laborers; co-laborers became friends. Eventually I gave presentations myself. I told my story. I no longer was alone.

It wasn't just the community I gained. I gained understanding. I shared my own experiences. I was interviewed by so many NDE researchers I can't recall them all. I became passionate about trying to find out more about the phenomenon of near-death experiences, especially among children.

Child experiencers can never really explain the way it is for them. To them, they are normal. They don't know they are different. But an observer from the outside can detect traits, often shared by other children who have had an NDE. For example, money doesn't matter much. Accumulating is not important to us. We all are willing to sacrifice what we have. Helping people is a priority. It's as if it becomes part of our DNA. Another common trait: We are not afraid of dying. That is pretty universal among all experiencers.

We are not afraid of dying. That is pretty universal among all experiencers.

I created an IANDS chapter support group in the San Francisco Bay area where other experiencers could find people like them. Participants didn't even have to tell us their real names, if they didn't want to. They had a safe place to open up confidentially, tell their story, share problems, find assistance. We met once a month for fifteen years, and I met loads of people who have had near-death experiences. I also volunteered for a short time at the Mother Teresa house in San Francisco during the height of the HIV epidemic.

I eventually crossed paths again with Brinkley. He had started hospice work and serving veterans. Seeing an experiencer like him work with the traumatized and the dying confirmed my own sense of calling.

That's when I started to make connections between a near-death experience and post-traumatic stress disorder (PTSD) among veterans. It was integral to my making sense out of my own traumatic experiences, and eventually, to connect my life with what happened to Patrick.

My Third NDE

Sometime in 1999 my Angelstaff team and I were taking turns being present with a wonderful old lady who was in a nursing home and declining. We had been working with her and her family for a while. She was in and out of consciousness. One of us would sit next to her hospital bed and hold her hand, or we'd read aloud from a book we knew she liked. We played music she liked, very low in the background. We wanted to create a peaceful atmosphere in the room.

It was my turn to be with her. I sat in a green upholstered chair next to her bed. I could tell she had taken a turn; she was unresponsive. Still, my presence was something positive. I decided to close my eyes and meditate for a bit.

That's when I realized that I was not feeling very good myself. In fact, I felt awful and really hot all over. In a matter of seconds, I was perspiring so heavily that water was running down my face, into my eyes, all over my body. I was suddenly drenched!

I tried to get up. I didn't have the strength. I was gripped with fear. *Oh my goodness,* I thought. Then I realized something was happening, on top of whatever was going on physically. *Maybe . . .*

With eyes wide open, I could see myself in the chair. I was pulling the side of my hair and it glimmered, like a light. My hands were glowing. My entire body was shimmering!

Okay, I know exactly what this is. There was no reason to fight what was happening, so I just let go. I left this dimension. I was taken to another place. I knew *what* it was but I didn't know what to call it. Heaven? Perhaps. I do know that it was a special place, in eternity, where there is infinite wisdom and love. Where we are being cared for.

Almost immediately, a message came. Not a divine being, as in my first NDE, nor with a booming voice, as in my second NDE. But it was a clear message to my consciousness. I was given a choice. *Do you want to go home? Or do you want to stay?*

> *I was shown a life review. But it was not about me or my life. It was about humanity and life on earth.*

I knew, of course, that "home" meant beyond the veil—our real home, our home with God. And "to stay" meant to return to earthly existence.

I didn't communicate a reply right away. As I was trying to focus, thinking about what this thought meant, I was shown a life review. It wasn't like a series of images or scene after scene like a film. It wasn't like a dream either. It was something I was in. I was a participant.

This life review was not about me or my life either. It was about humanity and life on earth. I was shown the past, present, and future of the planet, the good and the bad. I was also shown the reality that we humans had a choice to make. There were two directions to choose from.

In the present review, I saw very clear pictures of what will happen to humans, to the planet, to the way of living, to the darkness coming upon us. Soldiers in crisis, families losing their homes.

The images gradually revealed a sky filled with a deep blood-red color; it was like nothing I'd seen before. I saw myself looking out a plane window onto a desert with that sky, overcome with a sense of loss. Then most of the scene and the people I could see became gray. Everything was gray, and I had an overwhelming feeling of darkness. Structures were almost skeleton-like. People were suffering but silent. I felt the emotions of the world's pain, frustration, and anger. And I sensed that this scene was moving up until the time where there was no way to turn around, to turn back. The darkness stayed for a long time.

This life preview reminded me that I played a part in this. A witness. And that's what happened. I became a witness on earth.

This vision was a choice between light and darkness. I decided that I had to go back. I had to do something about it.

Overcome by a Mysterious Illness

When I opened my physical eyes I was back in the green chair. I couldn't move. I knew I had a very high fever and was still feeling poorly. I knew that if I tried to get up I would fall.

Finally, my Angelstaff replacement arrived. She helped me out to my car. Even as ill as I was, I was stubborn and determined to drive myself home. But I did ask my colleague to dial my son. Of course, he pleaded with me not to drive and said he'd come and get me. I didn't listen. I don't remember the trip, but when I arrived home, I collapsed on the floor of the front room.

I think Bob took me to the hospital, but I'm not sure of all that happened. I ended up in the ICU. Even though I was half conscious, I do remember being wheeled in and hearing one of the doctors say, "Whoa, you shouldn't be alive." My fever was higher than 105 degrees. They put me on ice.

I was in the hospital for two weeks. They couldn't figure out what was wrong. I remember at least eight different doctors examining me, some from Stanford University, some from San Jose University, all wrapped up in protective gear. All their tests and theories led to nothing.

I certainly had time to mull over my latest NDE. I was experiencing trauma, the aftereffects. Nothing would be the same—again.

After I got home, I called an NDE researcher I had become friends with. I trusted her, so I told her what I witnessed. I wanted to try to make sense of this experience. She said she would think about it and call me back. Sadly, she didn't know what to make of it.

> *After my latest NDE I was experiencing trauma, the aftereffects. Northing would be the same again.*

With my involvement in IANDS and as the owner of Angelstaff, I had quite a few speaking engagements, focusing on this world's best practices of living and dying. Up to this point, I had not lectured to the public about my NDEs. If anyone asked, I wouldn't deny that I had had the experiences, but I didn't bring them up.

However, after this last NDE I began to briefly mention some of the visions. My aim was to motivate people toward choosing life, choosing the light. But many listeners got angry. I decided people didn't want to hear, so I stopped talking about what I had seen.

Time passed. The world moved on toward the first Gulf War, the dreadful September 11, 2001, terrorist attacks on the United States, the invasion of Iraq.

And it changed everything for my family and me.

A Fateful Decision

Patrick was grown now, in his thirties, married to Sylvia, and father to Patrick Junior and Janessa. He had a successful job as a manager at an auto body business. But when 9/11 happened, he was filled with righteous anger.

"Mom, I have to do something about this," he said. The next day he enlisted in the Army National Guard. He thought he could serve his country if there were any other domestic attacks, yet also stay close to his family. He wrote letters to Sylvia and me, explaining his choice to enlist.

I don't think he ever imagined that he would be deployed. After three years the growing demands of the Iraq War kicked in the "backdoor draft"—a practice in which active-duty personnel have their tours extended, reservists are called up, and national guard members are sent overseas.

When I heard that President Bush had ordered guards to Iraq, with Patrick being one of them, Patrick and I had a very frank conversation. He had already made a connection between his involvement in the war and his foreknowledge from when he was fifteen that he would die young.

I had no answer to the question he asked me: "Mama, am I going to die there?"

The weeks sped by before Patrick had to ship out. A few days before his departure, he and I were sitting on a bench at the house, near the garden. It was warm and sunny, a moment in which it was hard to believe there was a war happening on the other side of the world.

"Mom," he said, "for as long as you're going to need me—you and Dad and my children—I will be back to watch over you."

I didn't think much of it at the time. It just sounded like something my loving, sensitive son would say to assure me.

He spent as much time with his family as he could. He wrestled with nine-year-old Junior and helped him with homework. Two-year-old Janessa clung to his side. They were always laughing.

An Oppressive Presence

Ever since hearing that Patrick was going to Iraq—and especially when he was there—I had trouble sleeping. Exactly two weeks before he was killed, I had spent what seemed like hours languishing in the stage where I wasn't asleep but not awake—that uncomfortable in between.

> *I felt a presence. It was something heavy, something cold, something dark. The air turned foul.*

My headboard was under a window. Light from the street shown through the blinds so that the room wasn't completely dark. As I was staring into the room, I felt a presence. It was something heavy, something I didn't like, something cold, something dark. The air turned foul.

At first I just thought, *Go away!* Then I felt a huge weight on my body. I couldn't breathe. I couldn't move. I couldn't scream. I couldn't turn. I couldn't do anything. My next thought was, *Mon Dieu, this thing is going to kill me!* I could see an indentation of weight on the bedspread. Whatever this presence was, it had a dimension to it. It wasn't just a spirit.

That's when I got angry. I was not scared; I was mad! I yelled, "If you're not from God, go away! If you're not from God, go away!"

It did! I could not believe it. I sat up and swung my legs onto the floor. I just sat there, thinking, *What happened? What just happened?* I walked to the living room and checked the clock. It was around three in the morning. *Oh goodness,* I thought. *I hope nothing happened to Patrick.*

I dialed Bob, my ex-husband, with whom I remained friends, and left a message for him to call me back in the morning and to let me know if Patrick had called him.

I did not sleep the rest of the night. The next day, I had trouble breathing. I have asthma. Usually it's under control, but if it gets bad, I have to go to the emergency room. I called my health provider and talked to the advice nurse. "What happened? Did something trigger your condition?" she asked.

I told her that something had happened the previous night, but I did not give her details. I also mentioned my son was deployed. "Well, you don't have to look any further," she said. "That's what it is."

She was partially correct. She recommended I come in for an examination. I didn't want to, but by the end of the day I was worse and had to. I drove myself to the clinic and received treatment.

That night, I was scared to go to bed. Once again, the stress and the breathing problem kept me half awake well into the early hours. And then once again, that cold presence returned to my room. Before I did anything else, I said a prayer out loud. Immediately the atmosphere cleared. What a great relief!

As with the night before, I had no idea what that presence was, other than an evil force toying with me.

A Sign in the Desert Sky

During the week before he was killed, Patrick called me every day. He believed his time was ending. He was very disturbed but matter-of-fact. He had a deep belief in God, but his family was everything to him and he didn't want to leave them behind. He said to me, "Mom, I'm not coming back. It's very close now and there is nothing we can do about it."

I couldn't say anything for a moment. Finally I whispered, "Don't say that. I just can't believe that."

He said, "Mom, don't let them forget me."

On June 21, 2004, I drove from my home in Tracy, California, eight hours down to the Mojave Desert community of Twenty-Nine Palms, California. My friend was under hospice care in a hospital in Yucca Valley and I wanted to visit her one last time.

The green light grew larger. I wasn't frightened. I was in awe. After a few minutes, it faded into blackness.

She had invited me to stay in her home while there. When I arrived, it was late at night. I discovered I had been given the wrong front-door key. I would need to try the back-door key. The only way into the backyard, however, was over a ten-foot chain-link fence.

I took off my shoes and gamely climbed the links. As I rested for a moment at the top, I looked up to the star-filled sky. There is nothing like the desert for revealing the magnificence of the heavens.

That's when I saw a dense spot of green light in the expanse. It grew larger. I had never seen anything like it. I wasn't frightened. I was in awe. Then a huge pressure gripped my chest, a pain that wrapped around my heart. After a few minutes, the green light faded into blackness. The pressure, though, did not go away.

I had no idea what had just happened, but I felt a sad, ominous premonition that lasted through the night. Once in my friend's house, her cat—which knew me—kept crying and would not leave me alone. I finally had to shut it in another room so that I could try to sleep.

Devastating News

On the next day, June 22, 2004, I went to the hospital to see my friend. As I was massaging her legs with lavender oil, my cell phone rang. I stepped into the hall. It was my daughter-in-law Sylvia, hysterical and sobbing.

"Sylvia, sweetheart, I can't understand you! Can you give the phone to someone else?" I said.

A male voice came on the line. What he told me sent me to the floor, curled into fetal position against the wall, screaming.

The man was one of the two California National Guard officers who had come to Sylvia's home that morning. He said that at a little after midnight Pacific time, my beloved son, Sgt. Patrick Robert McCaffrey Sr., age thirty-four, had been shot dead. It happened at precisely the moment I saw the green light in the night sky.

Of course, I returned to my home in Tracy right away, driving into the night and crying the whole way. I tried to sleep that night, but it was impossible.

The next few days were filled with family and friends paying their respects and newspeople wanting an interview. In the middle of all that, I received email from one of the infantrymen in Patrick's unit. Sylvia and Bob gathered around my computer to look at recent photographs sent in the email.

There was one of him providing first aid to a fellow soldier overcome with heat exhaustion. Another photo seemed to glow. It had been taken forty-five minutes before Patrick and his patrol was ambushed. He is sitting on top of his Humvee, holding a piece of apple and beautiful white flowers that Iraqi children had just given him. And there is a huge, warm, relaxed smile on his handsome face. He looks at peace.

> *The room became silent, then a scent of roses filled the air. "Mom, Patrick is here."*

As I silently wept, everyone in the room stopped talking. The room became silent. Then a scent of roses filled the air. Everyone looked at one another. Many had tears in their eyes. I turned to Sylvia.

"Mom," she said. "Patrick is here."

I would hold on to that thought through the coming horrible days and weeks as we dealt with the government and prepared to bury Patrick.

After a private memorial reception in his hometown, my beloved Patrick was buried on July 2, 2004, in Oceanside, California, near where his wife's family lives.

A Mother's Grieving Heart

Two months later I was suddenly stricken by another fever and rushed to the emergency room. Doctors said both lungs had collapsed. I was shocked. I also cried out with frustration: Why was I still alive and Patrick was not?

I would have taken his place with joy. But that was not the plan and I had to accept it.

I closed Angelstaff. I no longer had the heart to run it. I could not make myself train staff, volunteers, and family members anymore. Nor could I muster the strength to sit with the dying.

I was being called to a new mission as an anti-war activist and advocate for marginalized veterans, especially those with post-traumatic stress disorder. It was a calling I didn't want and wouldn't have chosen. I wanted to understand why Patrick—and other soldiers—had to die, why there is war, and how to prevent it.

My painful experience of searching for the truth around Patrick's death fueled in me a passion to help veterans. Because of the connection I saw between the trauma of NDEs and people with PTSD, I opened my home as well as my heart. I created a foundation in Patrick's name and spent years raising funds and advocating for vets.

A Visit in the Night

Every June 22, the date of Patrick's death, his friends, family members, and the veterans I was helping would gather to honor him. We usually would go to the wall monument where Patrick's special flag flies. The vets would hold an official ceremony. They made it a wonderful time, really.

In 2010 the house was full. I don't even know how many people were there. A few nights before the anniversary, I was awake in bed, trying to sleep. It took me years after Patrick's death to be able to sleep well. This night, it was well past midnight and I was lying in the dark, thinking, praying. Or maybe I was actually asleep. I don't really know for sure. Because the next memory is of something dreamlike.

Something or someone was in my room. The first clue was the aroma of aftershave. I recognized its spicy scent. It was one that Patrick would wear.

Then in the dark, I saw a human figure, one that felt very familiar. A man in a military uniform. But not just any man.

"Mom . . ." Patrick's voice filled my ears. Now I saw his hazel eyes, close to my face, staring into mine. "Mom, my son . . ."

> *Patrick's voice filled my ears. His face was close to mine. Was it a dream? Was it a visit?*

"Patrick! Is that you? What is happening?" I whispered. I felt frozen on the bed. My heart was racing. Patrick . . . in my room! Every fiber of my body wanted to jump up and wrap my arms around him.

"Mom! My son!"

Suddenly my room returned to its dull, dark gray. I sucked air into my lungs. Was there something wrong with fifteen-year-old Patrick Junior?

I reached for my phone. The screen read 3:30 a.m. The next three and a half hours before I could call Junior were excruciating. At 7 a.m. I dialed his mobile phone. "Junior! Are you all right?"

"Grandma? What's going on?" stammered Junior. "I'm fine."

I told him about the vision. He repeated that everything was okay, and we hung up. I also checked on his little sister, my granddaughter, and I talked with my daughter-in-law, Sylvia.

All day long I thought about what had occurred. Was it a dream? Was it a visit? What did Patrick mean?

Another Son to Care For

The night fell. I wondered if I would have another sleepless night. I tossed and turned and may have slept a little. But then my room was filled again with Patrick's presence and I was wide awake.

This time his voice had more of an element of urgency and maybe some irritation. Still, he said only, "Mom, my son. Mom, my son."

"I don't know what you want, Patrick!" I cried out. "What are you asking me to do?"

"Mom, my son. Mom, my son."

Then he was gone. I sat in bed for a while, trying to figure things out. In the morning I mentioned the vision to John, one of the veterans who lived with me.

"Oh well, it's Patrick's anniversary. It's something about him. You'll find out," he said.

I desperately hoped so.

Later that day the phone rang in the house. I answered it. A boy's voice was weeping and sniffling.

"Hello?" I said. "Who is this?"

More sniffling, a few deep breaths, and a smothered sob.

Finally, someone who I guessed to be a teenage boy said, "You don't know me, but I need to talk to you."

I waited.

"I just read online that he's dead! I—I . . . maybe you don't want to meet me but—I'm not your grandson, but I am your grandson . . . Anyway . . ."

"Hold it. Hold it," I said. "Let's take this from the beginning. Slowly now, tell me who you are and what you are talking about."

The young voice began to sound stronger. Rapidly he said, "I just turned eighteen, and my mom just told me who my dad was, and it's your son, Patrick. And I just found out that he was killed in Iraq, so I don't know what to do. I wanted to meet you, but maybe you wouldn't want to meet me. "

I quickly thought of Patrick's girlfriends in high school. Monique? It must be Monique. They went out together for a year and a half or so, and then she just disappeared, breaking Patrick's young heart.

"Of course I want to meet you!" I said. "What is your name?"

Florentino was his name—Tino for short. He said he and his mother lived south of us, in the Central Valley. They were willing to drive up. Could they?

> *I know I was sent back to earth all those decades ago to share a message of love.*

"Of course you can! I can't wait to meet you!" I said. "Patrick would have been so proud to know he had another son!"

But, of course, he did know.

When Tino and his mother arrived, I instantly recognized Monique and gave her a big hug. Tino took my breath away. He had his father's smile and his hazel eyes.

I am so grateful that Tino was brought into my life. He has built relationships with his half siblings, and we have grown very close. I will always be there for him. As Patrick wanted.

The Message of Love

My years of working with the dying in hospice, supporting experiencers, helping soldiers with PTSD, and serving as an advocate for homeless veterans are mostly behind me now.

Maman du Ciel sent me back to earth all those decades ago to share a message of love. The years have taken a toll physically, but I'm not done yet. I know I have something else to do, although I don't know what it is.

Today, I am very much at peace. Everything I have done in my adult life was based on the needs of somebody else, to help others. To love.

My Life since My Near-Death Experience

Nadia McCaffrey

My three NDEs have had an enormous impact on my life. What I experienced shaped me into the person I am today.

Q *How did your NDEs affect your life?*

A From childhood until adulthood, I kept trying to figure out what my mission was. When I fell into helping neighbors who were dying, I realized my firsthand knowledge of the love and light beyond our lives here gave me insight and I could bring comfort and peace. That developed into my work in hospice.

Then, after my son, Patrick, was killed in Iraq, I knew I had to help veterans. I was especially sensitive to homeless vets and those who had experienced post-traumatic stress disorder, because the effects of NDEs can often feel like PTSD.

I can say, though, that because of my experiences, I am afraid of nothing. I have no fear. I have experienced the love of God. My faith is very, very strong.

Q *Has the intensity of your NDEs lessened over the years?*

A I can recall each of my NDEs as if it happened yesterday. The memories are more real than life here on earth. The heartbreak and disappointment I always felt when I had to return did lessen over time. But I never lost the sense that heaven is where I belong. It is home.

I'm very sensitive to spiritual things. For example, so many signs have occurred since Patrick's death: his visits in dreams, his presence, his messages to let me know he is watching over me and his children. I am grateful.

Q For years you told no one of your NDEs. How did you feel once you went public?

A I never tried to convince people of my story—sharing my experiences was never about me. It became part of my calling, part of what I was sent back to do—to help others, to love. Once I realized that, I felt compelled to continue sharing what I witnessed, what I knew as truth.

I spend much less time working for homeless vets and helping soldiers who have PTSD, but I stay in touch with hundreds of people and encourage them as much as I can.

I am very much at peace with myself. There is always hope; no matter how stressful and dark it looks, there is always a light.

Heavenly Messages that Transcend Time and Place

By Charles Taylor, as told to C. Hope Flinchbaugh

◆ ◆ ◆

We were born to die and we die to live. As seedlings of God,
we barely blossom on earth; we fully flower in heaven.

Russell M. Nelson

G od's country." That's what some people call the area where I
grew up, the Appalachian Mountains of Virginia. I was raised
near where the famous country music star June Carter Cash
was raised. Our small home was nestled right beside my grandparents'
cottage, down a dirt road. I was an only child who enjoyed being outside in the farm-fresh air and discovering critters and plants in the natural forests. My family had a large garden that we tended the old-fash-
ioned way—by hand and with no pesticides. The harvest from our
garden provided wholesome meals on the family dinner table. Today,
people call that organic gardening. Back then, we called it survival.

My dad was a self-employed welder, and my mom worked as a nurse
in a doctor's office, but she helped my grandparents with planting in
her free time. My grandparents were sharecroppers. Together, they
planted and harvested crops on other people's land for a share of the

profits. They raised a lot of tobacco—which is a seasonal crop and a one-time-a-year payday. When my grandparents weren't in the tobacco field, locals hired them to plant family gardens.

Even before I was school age I spent most of my days next door with my dad's parents in their little three-room cottage or out in the fields playing nearby as they worked.

People said I was my grandfather's shadow. All I know is that I developed a powerful love for my grandfather. Most days he wore bibbed overalls with a button-down shirt underneath. He was over six feet tall, weighed about 160 pounds, and had salt-and-pepper hair, but to me he was ten feet tall and bulletproof!

I was my grandfather's shadow. I developed a powerful love for him.

I wanted to be part of everything my grandfather did. Around age four, I even started helping to set tobacco—transplanting the seedlings—in the fields.

Oftentimes I carried water to the workers, leaning to one side from the weight of my load, with the bucket dragging on the ground.

In my free time, I'd go fishing or run around in the woods for hours. I stayed with my grandparents more than I stayed at home, so if I came up missing at dinner, the first place my parents looked was Grandpa's. If nobody heard from me by dark, only then would they get worried.

One of the rules of living way out in the country is that you don't go into the woods without a gun, so by the time I was six, I knew how to handle a small rifle. I had to watch out for snakes and rabid animals, to be sure. But mostly the gun was there in case I fell and was too hurt to walk out—I could fire my gun and someone could find me.

My dad told the story of when he was younger and a rabid fox almost got him. He was going out to feed his dog. Lucky for him, the dog grabbed the fox in midair before it sank its teeth into my dad. Dad's story made us all tread a little more carefully, especially in the woods.

Although we lived in the Bible Belt in southwest Virginia, we didn't belong to a church and we didn't talk about God or religion. God wasn't the first thing on my mind every day. Most of the time I woke up thinking about my grandfather and what we would do together that day.

My earliest recollection of any religious conversation was from my pediatrician. When my mother took me to the doctor, he asked her, "Did you take him to Sunday school yet?" I don't know why the doctor asked about church. But doctors are smart, and maybe that's why my parents took me to church. I wanted to know what this church thing was all about, so I sat and listened to the preacher.

An elderly lady named Miss Viola sat down beside me and a bunch of other kids in the third row and handed me a coloring book and some crayons.

"Here, you can color while he's preaching," said Miss Viola.

I thought, *I could stay at home and color!*

I figured I should listen to Miss Viola, but I wanted to hear what the preacher was saying. So I sat there with a little coloring book on my knee and scrubbed the crayon back and forth like I was coloring while I listened to the preacher at the same time.

That preacher mentioned two words I will never forget—*eternal damnation.*

My eyes got wide as saucers. I didn't know what that meant, of course, but he was so fired up that I knew it must be important.

Miss Viola leaned over and whispered to me, "Don't pay attention to the preacher. He's saying bad words."

"Why is the preacher saying bad words?" I asked.

A strange look passed over Miss Viola's face. "You need to go," she said.

I think she was trying to protect me from preaching on hell, fire, and damnation, but I liked the pastor and his preaching. However, I decided if I had to color every time I came to church, I didn't want to come back. But if I'd get to listen, that would be okay.

Today I realize that both the preacher and Miss Viola meant well. At least Mom could tell the pediatrician that I went to church!

A Student of Faith

My world came crashing in around me when I went to school. I had always suffered from severe car sickness, but when school started, it got worse, probably because I was in the car so much. From kindergarten through second grade, my mother drove me to school in a neighboring county because it was a shorter drive. But starting in third grade, I started going to school in the county we lived in. I arrived at school so sick that I could barely pay attention to what was going on. Worse, I knew what the ride home was going to be like. I did just what I had to do to survive school. Luckily, school came pretty easy for me. I picked up quickly on new subjects, and I breezed through my homework. In fact, I was bored a lot because I found schoolwork so easy.

When I was in fourth grade my teacher came to me one day and gave me some special problems. She said, "Here, Charles. I want you to answer these math, English, and spelling questions." I turned the papers in to her the next day. After grading the papers she told my parents and me that my work was far above grade level. She even talked to the high school principal and suggested that I skip the rest of elementary and middle school and go right to high school. Because the school district's high school class was full, however, I couldn't be enrolled.

Meanwhile, I continued to go to church with my parents and grandparents. I definitely saw my need for God like never before as I continued to struggle with car sickness and school. The Lord touched my heart and I was born again at age seven during what was called a roundup in church. I guess it got its name because everybody rounded up friends and family and got them into church to hear the gospel. At that point I knew what was right and wrong and I

> *The Lord touched my heart and I was born again at age seven during a roundup in church.*

wanted to see all my family again in heaven. I wanted to be saved, and that day, in church, I started my personal walk with Jesus.

My parents believed in God by now, too, and most Sundays they took me to Lime Hill Baptist Church. But my faith was energized mostly by my grandfather. Grandpa owned one suit, but he didn't need more than one because he rarely went to church with us. As I grew older, I was still my grandfather's shadow. Wherever my grandfather went, I wasn't too far behind. We grew everything we ate, so when he was in the garden working, I was beside him cultivating, planting, weeding, or harvesting. When I wasn't in school, I helped him in the tobacco fields.

I will never forget the night my grandfather was saved. His friends invited him to go to their church that night, but I wasn't there. I was at home inside our house when I heard this racket outside. I could hear my grandfather yelling and shouting even before I heard his vehicle coming! It kind of scared me at first. I thought somebody was hurt or needed help. I didn't know what was going on.

> *I said, "God, if you would take me on a tour of heaven, I'd like that."*

My parents and I ran to the door. Somebody else was driving and Grandpa was hanging halfway out of the vehicle on the passenger side, preaching at the top of his lungs. When we stepped outside, the car stopped and he leaped out of the car and came running up, preaching all the way like we couldn't believe! I mean the Spirit of God was all over the man. There was no doubting that. I could feel it. I had never seen my grandfather like that.

I remember his friends from the Gardeners Chapel Church took him around so he could tell the priest, the preacher, and anybody and everybody who would listen to how Jesus saved him.

After that, Grandpa said to me, "Charles, I want you to follow in my footsteps."

I knew he was talking about his faith. He wanted me to follow him in faith. I looked up to him and I started to consider my walk with God more carefully. One time on TV I heard a preacher talk about heaven and people who saw heaven. I prayed right then and there and asked God to let me get a glimpse of heaven.

I said, "God, if you would take me on a tour of heaven, I'd like that."

I didn't know then that God would take me up on that offer, both in a dream and in a near-death experience as an adult.

A Powerful Influence

One day in May when I was fourteen years old, I was working at a garden site with my mom, grandmother, and grandfather. Grandpa and I ran the tiller while Mom and Grandma did the planting.

The tiller was almost out of gas, so Mom and Grandma were going to go to the store to get gas. I told my grandpa, "I'll finish tilling. You can go get cooled off and get a drink."

Grandpa said, "No, you go ahead. I'll finish here."

We were gone maybe ten minutes. I'll never forget rounding the curve in the road on the way back. As soon as we turned that corner, I saw Grandpa sitting on the bank, looking up in the sky. To this day I can still see him like that, and I wonder if the good Lord told him his time was close.

We finished up the garden that evening and went home. When we got home, Grandpa and I sat in the living room. He said his back was hurting between his shoulders and asked me if I would rub some ointment there. I did but then had to go home to do some homework.

It was the middle of May and all the windows were wide open. I was home for maybe five minutes when I heard a loud thud. I got up and took off at a dead run.

My mom and grandmother were working in the garden on the other side of the creek. They heard it too. When I came around the corner of the house, I saw Grandpa lying there with his feet sticking out the kitchen door. He had stepped out onto the front step, but then fell backward. That thud was him hitting the floor.

I got to him and checked him. He didn't have a pulse. I started CPR. My mom and grandmother got there. Mom, a nurse, took over CPR for me.

"Call an ambulance!" she said.

I ran back over to my place because my grandparents didn't have a phone. I picked up the phone. We had a party line back then, and two neighbors were talking. I yelled, "Get off the phone! I've got to call an ambulance!"

They started asking me questions. Finally I told them what was going on so they'd get off the phone.

When I got back to Mom, all I heard was my grandmother screaming, "Do something for him! Help him!"

I can hear her to this day. Sometimes it still gets to me.

It took forever for the ambulance to arrive—about thirty minutes. I did CPR again while my mom met the ambulance.

The ambulance crew pulled me back and checked him. They declared my grandfather dead on the spot.

My mother told me just recently that while I went in to call the ambulance, she had revived him.

He lifted his head and said, "I was gone. Why did you bring me back? I was home."

He laid his head back and smiled, and then he was gone again.

I was devastated. I was instantly so homesick for him. It's hard to explain the kind of pain I felt inside. I ached to see my grandfather again and walk the garden together with him just one more time. As the sharp edge of grief diminished with time, I began to think about heaven and the afterlife. What was it really like? Did Grandpa see Jesus already? Was he happy, *really* happy, there? Did he ever think about me or want to talk to me as much as I wanted to talk to him?

Overcoming Pain

The car sickness I experienced as a child gradually subsided, especially when I learned to drive a car myself. Even though I excelled in school, I still didn't want to be there and was glad when it was over. After graduation, I immediately got a job working for a natural gas company. The company was founded during the Civil War and thrived because everybody got their salt there during that era. It has since changed ownership and names several times.

I never lost the work ethic that Grandpa modeled before me, and I worked all sorts of jobs for the natural gas company for twenty-two years.

The first few years I worked there, I handled barrels full of chemicals. With some other guys I worked with, we lifted barrels weighing three to four hundred pounds to get them on the truck, using cables and winches as needed. It was brute work, but I was in my early twenties and able to handle it. I pretty much worked a lot and slept a little.

> *I never lost the work ethic that Grandpa modeled before me.*

One night around two in the morning I was unloading a truck. I needed to use a 1,000-pound winch on an oil rig to unload 634 pounds on the truck. The cable on the winch wasn't long enough to reach the trailer bed, so I had to drag it back there. The third time I grabbed the cable and pulled it, I felt a crunch in my back. I didn't tell anyone what happened because I was afraid they'd fire me.

The pain in my back got worse and worse. At one point, I had to sit up in bed for two hours before getting up in the morning. At that time the company didn't have a lot of orders so I was able to keep my injury hidden.

One day at work I pulled out onto the highway. Because of my back pain, I couldn't turn my head to look at what was coming and almost got hit by a vehicle. That was when I knew I had to go get something done.

That night I set my alarm clock two hours early to allow for the two hours to get up. I woke up in the morning and couldn't feel anything from my waist down. I pushed down on my hips and finally my back popped and feeling came back. I decided I'd go to the hospital. I didn't want to end up paralyzed in a wheelchair for the rest of my life.

I went to the emergency room. The technicians took an X-ray of my spine. The doctor looked at the X-ray and said I had gas. I couldn't believe it!

The pain never let up. My neighbor was a chiropractor and eventually I went to him to see if he could help. He took a couple of X-rays. From the front, the screen didn't show anything. From the side, one vertebra looked turned upside down.

He looked at me, eyebrows raised. "So, when did you break your back?"

I had no idea my back was broken.

The chiropractor kept doing adjustments on me and told me it would get worse before it got better. It got a little worse. The adjustments eventually lessened the pain, but my back never healed completely.

A Chance Encounter

Back at work, we got in some lighter material that would be easier to load. Thankfully I got hurt on the tail end of the heavy and hard work.

A few months after my back injury, in August 1996, I was on an emergency run to get a part for a compressor that had broken down.

I stopped at a gas station in Wise, Virginia, to top off my gas tank because I still had about eighty miles to go. There was a wall of Plexiglas between me and the cashier, but that didn't stop me from noticing her.

I thought, *Wow, that's the most beautiful girl I ever saw in my life.* What I didn't know is that this college girl with the long blond hair and shy smile would one day pray me back from the brink of death.

I gave her my money and left. But for the next eighty miles, I couldn't get her off my mind.

When I arrived at my destination to buy the part I needed, I told my friend Boomer, "Man, I just saw the most beautiful girl I ever saw in my life."

He said, "Really? Where at?"

"At the Exxon station, where I just filled up my truck," I answered. "Man, I just couldn't believe it."

> *What I didn't know is that this girl would one day pray me back from the brink of death.*

On the way back to work, traveling down the same highway with the new part I needed, I was still thinking about her. I decided to top off my tank with gas and see if she was still there. I quickly filled my tank and went up to pay for my gas. She had her back turned to me and the first thing I noticed was her long hair. She had long blond hair all the way down to her backside. I saw the college books lying there in front of her. She was studying while waiting on customers. When she turned around, I saw that beautiful face and thought, *Oh my goodness. I'm going to ask her out!*

I was twenty-four years old and she was nineteen. Her name was Angela. She gave me her phone number, and I guess you could say the rest is history.

In Angela's Words: A Vision from God

Even when I was young I knew God was real. I begged my parents to let me go to the nearby Baptist church, and I actually walked there every time the doors were open.

My body began to develop early, by age ten. Most days when I got off the school bus, I was met by girls and then boys who teased me, snapped my bra, and made up false stories about me. By the time I was in high school, I was a victim of a lot of bullying and, in time, even contemplated suicide. I was so lonely.

> *I asked God for proof that I was going to fall in love with somebody who loved God.*

I prayed every night because my life was so hard back then. I wondered if I'd ever have a boyfriend who was kind. I asked God for proof just to know for sure that I was going to fall in love with somebody who was good and loved God.

One night as soon as I went to sleep, I dreamed about a very bright place, and I knew that I was in the presence of the Lord. I knew it was God our Father. In front of Him was a man who looked almost like a statue. He came toward me. I woke up and right then and there, and I thanked the Lord for that dream because I knew that the man I saw in that dream was going to be my soul mate. I asked God to help me, to guide me on whom to actually marry.

I was working at a gas station part-time. One day I looked out beyond the gas station counter and saw a man hop out of his company truck.

He had on a work shirt, a cap, and dark safety glasses. His shoes were untied with the tongues sticking out. He was grimy from work. All I could see was his little tiny nose at the end of his face because his beard came all the way up to the glasses. I mean, I couldn't even see his cheeks or his eyes, but I could tell he had been working, and I could tell he was tired.

Something within me made me write down my phone number and agree to go out with him.

Later on I wondered, *Could this be the man I had prayed about? Was he God's choice for me?*

Some of the boys who harassed me in school were rich. I didn't want somebody who was rich. In fact, I wanted nothing to do with money. I wanted a hardworking man, not afraid to get dirt on his fingers—a real man like my dad, who is a mechanic.

As I got to know Charles, I felt a spiritual connection. I just knew that he was my other half. Eventually I believed that Charles was the man who God showed me in the dream.

Charles's Need for Change

Angela and I gradually fell in love, but we barely had time to date. We were workaholics—we both worked two to four jobs each during our courtship. Whenever she could, Angela visited me on my lunch break at work. I looked forward to each conversation. Occasionally we found time to go out together when our work schedules agreed. I was always on call, so it wasn't unusual to go out on a date but get called back to work within an hour. When we finally did get together, we always had a great time.

Angela and I dated for a long time—for years actually. I knew that my smoking bothered her asthma, but I couldn't seem to stop. Some of the guys at work joked around that I was the Marlboro mouse, referring to that old billboard advertisement of a mouse in a cowboy hat, puffing on a cigarette.

I was addicted and I knew it. My grandfather was no longer around to talk to, but God was still with me. One night He set me straight by appearing to me in an incredible dream in which He let me see heaven.

A Dream of Heaven

I have no recollection of traveling through space or time or anything like that during the dream. I just knew that I had crossed the Jordan River and I was standing in the most beautiful place I had ever seen.

I used to skydive and the dream reminded me of doing it, of how you land. Before you touch the ground, you pump the brakes on the parachute so it goes up, allowing you to hit the ground softly, taking a couple of steps until you are on solid ground.

> *One night God appeared to me in an incredible dream in which He let me see heaven.*

My dream started off like that, but without the parachute. In the dream I flew over the Jordan River and had forward momentum as I floated down. I took three steps and then came to a stop. I landed in this beautiful field. There were people everywhere. An angel stood on my right side, and my back was to the Jordan River.

I saw so many people talking to one another in little groups, some off in the distance. I somehow knew they were friends and relatives who had already passed on. Some of these people had lived generations before me and even before my grandpa. Even though I could see them, I was told that I wasn't there to meet them.

I looked to my left and saw a tree on a little ridge on a hill about two hundred yards away. I wondered, *What kind of tree is that?*

Suddenly the tree answered my question! The answer appeared like one of those callouts on a page in a book—a round circle with words in it. A small round circle came up to me. The leaves and the fruit came right up to my face and I knew the kind of tree it was. I forget what it "told" me. I saw and heard many things that I can't recall now because they weren't meant for me to remember back here on earth, but to enjoy while I was in heaven.

The angel on my right started talking and that's when I saw him. *Grandpa!* He looked so happy! My grandfather ran up to me on my right side. I was thrilled to see him!

The angel turned to my grandfather and said, "No, it's not his time."

After he said that, my grandfather went back the other way. Even though our connection was brief, it was there and I didn't feel sad. It did my heart good because now he knew I was in heaven and I knew he was there too. It was an incredible experience. I knew that he was where he belonged. Even though I knew I wasn't going to stay there, that brief encounter gave me a sense of peace and hope.

I looked out over the field where I stood. Flowers of indescribable colors swayed in breezes that were encased in music. Songs of praise permeated all throughout heaven. I heard the music all around me, like surround-sound stereos on earth, and the heavenly choruses sent chills down my spine.

In another memory of this dream, I was in a very bright, quiet room and I saw two angels standing in front of me facing each other. I don't know how I got there. The angels were talking to each other. I couldn't hear them, but I knew they were talking about me.

The next thing I knew, Jesus was standing in front of me, a little to my left.

Jesus . . . He was amazing. The feeling of being next to Jesus was love, nothing but pure, saturating love. There's no other way to describe it.

Jesus said to me, "You have to quit smoking."

Well, I didn't want to quit smoking. He knew that. But He told me if I didn't, that something bad would happen. I didn't care about what would happen to me, but Jesus knew my weak spot. When He said that something bad would happen to Angela if I didn't stop smoking, it made me pay attention. Angela has severe asthma, and secondhand smoke bothered her a lot.

> *The feeling of being next to Jesus was love, nothing but pure, saturating love.*

As I paused and considered Jesus's words, He activated a video to my right. The video was presented in higher definition and color than anything we have on earth today. On the screen, I saw Pastor John Hagee preaching a message about Job and how God put Job to the test. The pastor and all the people that go to John Hagee's church stood in front of me on the screen; they couldn't have been any more vibrant and clear.

I believe there are certain things that God allows to happen. In this case, the bad that could happen would hinge on my decision to smoke or not to smoke.

After seeing the message in that room, the next thing I knew, I was walking down a street in heaven with Jesus. There was a wall built alongside the road. I jumped up onto the wall, having the time of my life. Jesus held my right hand with His left. I looked over at Him and I just knew He marveled at how a grown man my size behaved like a five-year-old kid. I walked, bounced, jumped, and had a blast on the wall! I loved laughing and carrying on without any pain whatsoever. I had no fear of falling down off the wall and getting hurt. No sadness. I experienced the most unbelievable feeling of peace. I'd never felt peace like that before, and I know it is peace that only God can give.

Before I left, Jesus picked up a stone. He handed it to me and I looked at it, knowing He gave it to me with a special purpose. The stone was the most beautiful blue sapphire, as big as the palm of my hand.

Jesus said, "This is yours when you return."

Now, I don't know what that meant. I just know He meant for me to have that stone when I return to heaven one day. I don't know why it is significant to the Lord, but it is. Evidently, whenever I go back to stay, I'm going to have a sapphire. How wonderful is that?

A Change Reimagined

When I woke up the next morning, I had to face Jesus's words from my dream and determine what I was going to do. I wasn't a coffee person. My daily routine consisted of smoking three cigarettes and drinking a liter of Mountain Dew first thing in the morning. I'd just spent $200 the day before to buy about three cartons of cigarettes. But the next thing I knew, I was jumping up and down on all the cigarettes because I didn't want anything bad to happen because of my addiction to them.

I said to God, "I quit, but I can't do it without Your help."

God answered that prayer. It is extremely hard to quit smoking cold turkey like that.

The first time I really wanted a cigarette, I immediately prayed, "Lord, help me. I've got a craving for it." The craving lasted two or three seconds and then it was gone.

The desire happened one more time and that was it. Jesus delivered me from nicotine and kept me from causing hurt or pain to the one I loved, my dear Angela.

It was around this same time in 2007 that God taught me a lesson I'll never forget, a lesson about forgiveness. I was on my way home from work one day and I had to pull off the interstate, because my stomach was in so much pain and I was bleeding profusely from my rectum.

> *The message the Lord gave me is that we must forgive people.*

My thirst was outrageous, and I wanted to drink anything in sight. I had an old bottle of pain medication in the black box in my truck, a bottle I'd kept there just in case of injury. I always kept something in case I got hurt or something like that and needed it. The bottle was about eight years old, but I took the meds anyway.

I drove myself to the emergency room and wrote down "internal bleeding" as my reason for being there. I didn't know if that was true, but I was guessing. They wheeled me back to a room and started an IV. I was so thirsty and kept asking for a drink. I drank everything I could get my hands on all night long. I mean, I looked over at a mop bucket while I was lying there in the hospital bed and thought, *Man if I get to that mop bucket, I don't care what they'd mopped up. I want to drink every bit of that water.* As I lay there, I was given pint after pint of blood and fluids.

At that moment, the Lord said to me, "Now, you know what *thirsty* is. When I was dying on the cross, I said, 'I thirst,' and they gave me the bitter cup to drink. What did I do? I said, 'Father, forgive them for they know not what they do.'"

The Lord told me that we have to forgive others or else our Heavenly Father will not forgive us for our sins. Here was the Creator of all the earth's springs of water. He grew the grapes and everything else, yet those people wouldn't give Him a decent drink. All Jesus ever did was perform miracles, raise the dead, heal those who were sick, and come to save the world—not to condemn it. Even though He had done no wrong, they wouldn't even give Him something to drink when He was dying. Yet He asked His Father to forgive them.

The message He gave me is that we must forgive people. Even if you've done no wrong and people have not treated you right, you still have to forgive them because like He said, how can the Heavenly Father forgive you if you don't want to forgive others first for their transgressions?

I went into surgery the next morning and the doctors found a blood vessel that had burst. They took care of that and I am completely recovered.

Starting a New Life

Angela and I have both faced quite a bit of sickness in our lives. Around the same time that I had surgery for a burst blood vessel, Angela was diagnosed with fibromyalgia, a debilitating and painful disease that really set her back. But we think of it this way: We try to set an example of praising God through all of our hardships.

Angela and I agreed that we would marry once and only once in our lifetimes, so we wanted to get it right. Our courtship and engagement combined lasted thirteen years. We each kept hectic work schedules even while planning our wedding. We didn't want to live together before getting married. We really wanted to do this right, so we needed to shop around for a house. Angela's brother found a place, and she was so excited about the little house he found. I didn't care so much about the house. I was looking forward to being married and living together under one roof.

We decided that Angela would move into the house first and I would move in after our wedding. Our wedding date was set for November 28, 2009. Angela loved making the wedding plans and we dreamed of finally being husband and wife. In fact, I was thrilled about being married to her, and on October 15, 2009, I called Angela on the phone.

"Hey, Angela, what do you think about getting married today? About seven o'clock?"

In Angela's Words: Listening to God

Charles totally surprised me this time. I paused a minute. My parents were helping me move in and helping me plan the wedding for November. I felt like their feelings needed to be considered.

Finally I answered, "I've got to ask Mom and Dad if they mind us getting married today."

I talked to my parents and it turned out that my dad had a dream the night before that he said seemed so real. In the dream, Charles and I got married in a church he hadn't seen before and the service was officiated by a pastor he'd never met. He said that Charles and I were not dressed in our wedding clothes, but normal church clothes. It amazed me that God would give my dad a detailed dream like that on the night before Charles called me. Wow!

As if that wasn't enough confirmation, October 15, 2009, was my parents' thirty-third wedding anniversary! They thought that having our wedding on their anniversary was a great idea.

Now I had to consider how I felt. My wedding dress was having alterations made. There was no way Charles could rent a tux in a couple of hours. How could we pull together a wedding in three hours?

But I was invested in much more than the wedding itself. I wanted to move into this cute little house and live as husband and wife *immediately*. I'd been waiting for this for thirteen years, so I didn't turn it down. I said YES!

I called the preacher we wanted to officiate the wedding, then I ordered the cake. In three hours, our family got the preacher, the church, the cake, and the flowers, and decorated the reception

> *I asked the Lord to tell me which man is the right person and to make sure I have the right one. He did!*

hall. Except for two people, everyone who was on the original guest list for the November wedding was present. Due to the late notice, we were married in a church that my dad had never seen before and the pastor was someone my dad had never met. My wedding dress I bought for $700 was being altered and wouldn't be ready for a couple of weeks. So I wasn't wearing a wedding dress, and Charles didn't have a fancy tux. But it didn't matter. We knew we were in the will of God and He set everything up. I asked the Lord to tell me which man is the right person and to make sure I have the right one. He did! We dressed up in our Sunday church clothes and got married!

We were two happy newlyweds! We couldn't travel a lot because I was still struggling with pain from fibromyalgia, but we celebrated birthdays and holidays at local family gatherings and enjoyed each other's company.

On our days off, if we had no other plans, we spent our time recording CDs for missionaries, evangelists, and everyday Christians who live in other nations. We found a website called Life Lessons. People who posted on that site were hungry for the Word of God and good teaching. Charles knows Ray Comfort, so we got his permission and sent off many of his CDs to Africa, Spain, Italy, South America, and Europe. Charles and I shipped between fifty and one hundred CDs worldwide.

My faith was challenged when I was alone one night in my kitchen when I heard God speak to me.

The year after we were married we traveled to Gatlinburg, Tennessee, to the Smoky Mountains to celebrate the Fourth of July. The celebration was a lot of fun, and Charles and I had the time of our lives passing out CDs to people there.

But my faith was challenged when, less than three years after the wedding, I was alone one night in my kitchen when I heard God speak to me.

He said, "Do you want the one you love to come back to you?"

I got on my knees and cried out to God to bring Charles back to me.

Charles's Story: Facing Death

From 1992 through 2012, I worked night shift every other month for a natural gas storage company. The plant was manned 365 days a year, day and night. We mined salt out of huge underground caverns, which were about three thousand to four thousand feet deep. We pumped water down into one end of the cavern and then pumped it out the other end. After the water came out the other side of the salt mine, it was at 100 percent salinity, which means we couldn't get any more salt in the water. When "the brines," or salt water, were mined out at 100 percent solution, we pumped it into three big ponds that were from three to twelve acres. These were holding ponds for the salt plant. The salt in those ponds would be made into kosher salt, table salt, road salt, and ice salt.

After the salt was removed, we then stored natural gas in the empty caverns. We had contracts with different utilities and other places that supply directly to homes and businesses. A company we supplied could call anytime and demand fifty million or five hundred million cubic feet per day as a flow rate, and we were prepared to give them what they needed. My position as a mine supervisor was to do pre-ship inspections. I loved my job, but it was physically demanding as well as mentally taxing. Believe it or not, there was a defibrillator machine on the walls of the offices at the plant because the job was that stressful.

We worked with hydrogen sulfide (H2S), which is a high concentration of poisonous gas used during the drilling and production of crude oil and natural gas. A certain level will render you unconscious and more will kill you. When on certain jobs, we had to work with special gear that looked a lot like scuba gear. You could make one mistake and it would be your last mistake. We had all heard stories of workers who were injured or even died from handling the substances.

Fibromyalgia had hit Angela so hard by this time that she was mostly confined at home. My company was about forty miles away from home, so I left around six o'clock in the evening and didn't return until eight o'clock in the morning.

We did all right financially on my paycheck with one vehicle between us, so while I worked all night at the natural gas company, Angela cleaned the house, prepared meals, and rested in between to help ease the pain she was in. I wasn't allowed to receive any phone calls from home, even on lunch breaks. That was the toughest part for both of us. We liked to keep in touch, but we abided by company rules and refrained from any personal calls until I was on the road, on the way home.

> *We couldn't call each other, but the communication was right there, in a sweet note.*

The highlight of my workday was opening my lunch box. Most days I had a bologna and cheese sandwich in there, my favorite. But I always dug deeper into my lunch box to find the note or the little surprise Angela put in there for me. We couldn't call each other, but the communication was right there, in a sweet note that said, "I love you" or "I miss you, can't wait until you come home." It was like opening a Christmas present every day! Angela waited up for me all night and had a meal waiting for me when I walked in the door. I didn't ask her to do that. She just did it out of love for me.

On the night of February 27, 2012, I finished my rounds at work and went from the main office back into my little office to do some paperwork. No one else was in the building. As I walked in the door, I noticed my work cell phone was going dead. The battery was dying, so I walked around my large L-shaped desk to a small charger box that was mounted to the wall and plugged in my phone. As I walked around the tip of the long side of my desk, sharp pain hit me in the chest, radiating up through the right side of my neck and into my jaw.

Am I having a heart attack? The pain was so intense, it scared me. I stumbled around the desk corner to my office chair, which was one of those that rock, roll, and recline. Pain and numbness tingled down my right arm. I staggered a bit, but I made it to the chair and sat down. I thought, *This is not good—I need to get my feet up.* I threw my feet up on my desk and reclined the chair back as far as it would go, believing that if I got my feet up, it would help me somehow. And that's the position I was in when I died.

In Angela's Words: Praying for a Future

I had just finished dusting and was thirsty and hungry. I was on my way to the refrigerator for something to eat when the Holy Spirit came upon me and spoke really loud and with so much power that his voice rumbled throughout my whole body. It was so scary. I can't say it any other way. It was so intimidating. I instantly got on my knees. I mean, I cannot get on my knees for anything now. Even with pillows, it feels like I'm kneeling on broken glass. But that day and at that moment, I did not feel the pain. I did not even question getting down. I knelt before the living God, crying, praying, my heart pounding. I didn't know what was happening, but I knew God was talking to me.

God said, "Angela, I need to know if you want your loved one to come back to you."

I thought in my mind, *Well, who is the loved one?*

So I started praying. I said, "Lord God, please, who is it? My husband or my parents? Who is it? What's wrong?"

I knew something was wrong.

God said, "They are here with Me in heaven right now."

So that means they're dead, I reasoned. By now I was crying and going on. I prayed and prayed. God didn't say anything about my husband until I prayed. Finally, when I was finished praying, I knew. I knew it was for my husband. I don't know how long my prayers lasted because I had no sense of time as I poured out my heart to God. By now I knew that Charles was in trouble and God wanted me to pray.

Charles's Visit to Heaven

Next thing I knew I was traveling above my desk, my office, and the plant at a 45-degree angle. I am more sure about what I saw and felt that night than anything I've ever experienced in my life. Once you pass away from this life and into the next, there is absolute knowledge and confidence in what you know. I knew there were two angels carrying me, one under each arm. We were flying upward, headfirst, and going extremely fast!

My angels were carrying me so fast that it reminded me of *Star Wars* or *Star Trek* when the spaceship goes so fast through the pitch-dark outer space that the stars going by look like little silver lines. I knew the angels were there, but I couldn't concentrate on them. At the moment, I couldn't take my eyes off the beautiful light that was ahead of me.

I used to do a lot of flying and what I felt was the same as flying a plane into a very rural airport. When you fly into remote places from a high altitude, you may see your destination far off in the distance. My flight toward heaven was like that. I saw this light way out in front of me and it grew brighter and more defined as we got closer to it. I believe this is the light at the end of the tunnel effect we hear so much about. I get why people say that.

Moments later, I could see a brilliant white bank of clouds ahead, the whitest of clouds with a light emanating from them. I was thrilled to enter into that wall of clouds because I *knew* what was on the other side—I knew the source of all that light was Jesus! Glory to God! We flew right into those clouds, headfirst.

I wanted to see the angels who were transporting me, but I couldn't take my eyes off of Jesus.

One moment later, we broke through the white clouds to the other side. I looked to my right.

Jesus!

Angels still carried me, one underneath each arm. By now I wanted to see the angels who were transporting me, but I couldn't take my eyes off of Jesus. Jesus rode the prettiest white horse I have ever seen. He rode like lightning across white unsullied clouds, from my right to my left. My angels and I traveled toward Him.

I was mesmerized. The Lord and Creator of heaven and earth rode like the wind. As soon as we were close to Him, He looked over at us, held out His left hand, and said, "It is not your time."

Instantly, we were traveling backward at what seemed to be light speed. At first I was going backward on my back, but somewhere along the way back we did a barrel roll of some sort and I flipped, flattened back out, belly to earth, and flew headfirst in that position back to earth.

In Angela's Words: Answered Prayer

It was important to God that I pray for my husband. That resounding voice rang in my ears and rumbled through my whole body.

"Do you want your loved one to return to you?"

I knew that if my loved one was returning, that meant that Charles had passed on. It scared me to think about that, but I was determined to answer God's question.

> God's resounding voice rang in my ears and rumbled through my whole body.

"Yes, yes! I want my loved one to be here with me. Please keep him here with me! Protect him. Don't let anything bad happen to him. If he died, then bring him back!"

I prayed, tears running down my face, and didn't stop until the peace came. I knew in my heart that God had answered my prayers. I also knew I was about to break the company rules. I was calling Charles immediately!

Charles's Story: A Peace Like No Other

I began to spiral slowly, headfirst, toward earth in an unhurried clockwise spin. I saw the entire facility where I worked, all six hundred acres! I flew downward toward my little office there. On the way down, I could see one other guy and his vehicle at the other building.

As I went through the roof, I saw a Cat5 internet wire going up through the insulation panels. I had no idea where it went, but that stuck in my mind because I didn't realize before that it was up there. It's funny how the things in the natural grab our attention. Of course,

I could see things in the natural from an entirely new perspective—the roof above my office's drop ceiling!

I went down through the drop ceiling tiles and saw my body lying back in my office chair, feet propped up, eyes closed. My head was centered on the chair's headrest. My right hand was on my chest and my left hand crossed over my right because I was holding my neck and jaw. It was surreal to see my body so lifeless, but it was exactly as I had left it, in the exact position. It was no more alarming to me than seeing a coffee cup by the coffee machine. I slowly floated downward.

I drew closer, belly to earth, but when I got so close to my body that I was about to kiss myself, I just rolled over and entered back into my body. I remember heaving that first breath, and I remember the pain. After being free of the pain, flying through orbit, and most of all seeing Jesus, I really did not want to stay. The pain was sharp and hadn't let up at all. What could I do? I struggled with the pain.

I don't know how long I was back in my body before I died again. The experience was almost a carbon copy of the first one. I was with angels and we were traveling through space at an amazing speed. The stars again zipped past, and we flew through that shining white wall.

Again, Jesus was riding His white horse, and again, He held out His hand. Only this time He said, "'I told you that your time has not yet come.'"

When I came back through the ceiling the second time and saw my body, I braced myself. I knew the pain I was in for when I entered my body again. In that moment, God let me know everything was going to be all right. A peace came over me like nothing on this earth I could ever imagine. I *knew* everything was going to be all right.

The phone rang. Somehow I managed to get up from my desk and unplug it from the wall.

In Angela's Words: A Message from God

When Charles picked up his work phone he was supposed to say the company name and then his own name and then, "How may I help you?" When I called him, he simply said, "This is Charles. How may I help you?" It wasn't Charles's normal voice, and I didn't think it was really him.

I said, "Who is this?"

"This is Charles."

"I've got a message from God above. It scared me to death. He said that you were with Him or something. What happened? Are you okay?"

He said "I kind of feel bad."

"What's hurting you?"

I waited and waited and waited. He finally told me he had to lie down in his chair and he had died. I begged him to go to the doctor, but in my heart, I knew God gave him back to me. So I had no question about whether or not he was all right. I knew he was going to be all right. But I could tell right then and there he was not in a fair state of mind. He could barely talk to me. So I begged him to go tell his coworker, and he said his coworker was in another building. He couldn't get to him. He couldn't even get up to walk.

I said, "Okay then, go to the hospital."

"I can't. I'm the only one here doing all the work."

We had only one vehicle at this time, and Charles had it. My parents were traveling and I had no one I could call. Charles didn't want to go to the hospital because he felt that God told him he would be fine.

I said, "But what about work? Your job doesn't really care what God said to you. You need to go to the hospital. You need to be checked out."

My husband insisted on waiting for his shift to end. I had no choice but to wait at home until he returned home or contacted me again.

Charles's Story: Living out the Promise of God

I feel sorry for anyone who says there is no God. When I died, I entered into heaven. I died twice the night I had the heart attack. While this was going on, my wife, who was at home forty miles away, had no idea what was happening with me, yet God told her to get down on her knees and pray for me like she had never prayed for me before. After she did this, she called me at work because she knew something was wrong. I answered the phone and she didn't recognize my voice. I was very weak and in a lot of pain. She asked me what was wrong. I told her what had happened and that I didn't feel good. I finished my shift and then went to the doctor. They ran tests on me and told me I had a heart attack.

I wasn't surprised about the diagnosis. But I also know without a doubt that on the night of the heart attack, God let me know everything was going to be all right. I knew He meant that I would go back to being a normal human being again with normal aches and pains, that my time had not yet come. I had heart surgery, fully confident in God's promise to me. I came through it okay and today my heart problem is gone.

My Life since My Near-Death Experience

Charles Taylor

I am in pain every day due to my broken back, but God has alleviated my suffering by putting Angela in my life. Other than my salvation, she is the best thing the good Lord ever gave me.

Q *Did your near-death experience help you to make sense of things that happened in your life when you were younger?*

A I was really carsick when I was younger. Although I was a good student, the sickness made my school experience pretty bad. My teachers thought I was really smart, but I didn't want to focus on doing great in school. But later in life I actually ended up being in the Triple Nine Society, the world's largest group designed for intellectual exchange for anyone with an above-average IQ. In simple terms, this meant that I was one of thirteen out of ten thousand people who scored above 145 IQ and who were considered profoundly gifted.

I realize that God gave me this gift. To me, I think I've proved the Scripture:

If any of you lacks wisdom, you should ask God, who gives generously to all without finding fault, and it will be given to you.

(James 1:5, NIV)

I thank the good Lord above for giving me the wisdom and knowledge so that learning comes easily to me.

Q *How do you know your near-death experience was real?*

A Angela and I went to Hobby Lobby one day for a painting class. As I left the store, I looked over and saw a large blue diamond-shaped stone. It was clear as glass. I bought it. This blue stone looked just like the sapphire in my dream. Obviously, I don't have any real sapphires the size of the palm of my hand, and this stone has a sharp edge on the back of it. But to me, seeing this stone was a sign that the sapphire in my dream was real.

Q *If you could have experienced one more thing or person as part of your NDE, what or who would it be and why?*

A There's a sadness in my life that I have to wait longer to see Grandpa again. Every year around my birthday, I visit my grandpa's grave. I still get choked up because I'm missing him, but then I think about his words after he began his walk with Christ: "Charles, I want you to follow in my footsteps."

After seeing him in heaven, I think he knows that I'm walking with God the best I know how. One day, one day soon, I will see him again. And the next time I hope to stay!

Q *How has your NDE affected your life today?*

A God has been part of my life since I was young, but now I make God a priority. He healed me and allowed me to witness His blessings. Not only is He the one I turn to in times of need, but He is also the one I thank for the good things in my life.

A Note from the Editors

We hope you enjoyed *Messages from Heaven,* published by Guideposts. For over 75 years, Guideposts, a nonprofit organization, has been driven by a vision of a world filled with hope. We aspire to be the voice of a trusted friend, a friend who makes you feel more hopeful and connected.

By making a purchase from Guideposts, you join our community in touching millions of lives, inspiring them to believe that all things are possible through faith, hope, and prayer. Your continued support allows us to provide uplifting resources to those in need. Whether through our communities, websites, apps, or publications, we inspire our audiences, bring them together, and comfort, uplift, entertain, and guide them.

To learn more, please go to guideposts.org.

We would love to hear from you:

To make a purchase or view our many publications, please go to shopguideposts.org.

To call us, please dial (800) 932-2145

Or write us at Guideposts, P.O. Box 5815, Harlan, Iowa 51593